Agent Rise

Real Estate Agent's Guide

To Building A Career You Love

Neil Mathweg

Agent Rise:
Real Estate Agent's Guide To Building A Career You Love
Copyright © 2021 Neil Mathweg
All rights reserved.

Cover design by Tingalls Graphic Design

Paperback ISBN: 9798481867700

*To my wife Jenny,
and to my children Natalie, Izzy, and Ashton
who have gone on this wild ride with me
building Agent Rise*

And thanks to Kyla Meuer and Dwight Clough for all their hard work on this book. Thanks to Keith Gilmore, Valerie Wilson, Mindi Kessenich, Paige Corbett, Dustin Brohm, and TJ McGraw for being earlier readers, proofing, and helping the book become what it has. And thank you to everyone in the Agent Rise Community who has supported and encouraged me along the way. Agent Rise wouldn't be what it is today, if it wasn't for this amazing community.

Table of Contents

Why I wrote this book for you......6

Part One: Mary's Story......9

   1. Trapped!......10

   2. Early signs of success......15

   3. Passed!......17

   4. 87% don't make it!......19

   5. Shiny object syndrome......23

   6. A business you love......26

   8. Your identity......36

   9. Your announcement Letter......40

   10. Sphere of Influence Pillar™......45

   11. Compete against yourself......50

   12. My friend listed with someone else!......53

   13. Chase Pillar™ & lead generation......56

   14. Matchmaking & lead conversion......63

   15. Stacking lessons......66

16. Cracking the open house code..................72

17. Systems..................78

18. Believing the plan and forming habits..................92

19. Attraction Pillar™..................97

20. Sphere of Influence 2.0..................108

21. Clarity, congruency, and consistency..................114

Part Two: Your story..................117

22. Your plan..................118

23. Simplify and Amplify..................120

24. Agent Rise Steps™..................122

25. Three Pillar Plan™..................124

26. Work according to your vision..................135

27. Discover your power..................141

28. Consistency..................148

29. Day Blocking..................152

30. Self integrity..................154

31. Set boundaries..................157

32. Information alone doesn't work..................162

Free Resources..................166

Here's to the Risers..................167

Why I wrote this book for you

I wrote this book to help new agents and agents who feel stuck—not new, but definitely not where they want to be.

I recall seeing a post in a real estate agent Facebook group asking, "What is a great book for a new real estate agent to read?" The most popular books noted were books that most new agent would struggle to wrap their heads around. In most cases they were too advanced, and, in the end, would only confuse a new agent.

I want this book to be the resource new agents pick up, read, get a framework from, and flourish to heights they dreamed of when getting into the business.

And I wrote this book to help put an end to the revolving door of real estate. For far too long I have seen agents come and go. People start in this business full of high hopes only to crash and burn months or years later. In fact, according to a 2014 NAR report, 87% of agents don't make it past 5 years! That's crazy, and it needs to end.

This book is divided into two parts. In Part One, we are going to bring you on a journey with Mary, a brand new agent with limiting beliefs, and an agent who lacked a clear plan. Mary is trying to figure out why all her hard work is producing no results. In Part One, you'll see coaching in action to understand how coaching helps remove limiting beliefs to lead you to breakthroughs you never imagined were possible. You'll also see Mary build a clear plan—congruent to her strengths, become consistent, and experience the results she desired. Then we move on to Part Two—Your plan. We'll walk with you to begin building your plan so you can get after the breakthroughs you are looking for.

You are a fighter, a survivor, an agent on the rise! I hear you, and I want to help you. I wrote this book for you. I want to see you reach your dreams. I believe in you and want to give you the guide you need to succeed.

Why do agents fail? Is it lack of information?

No! In fact, I think it's the exact opposite. I think what's leading agents to fail is information overload. We are smack dab in the middle of the information era. Agents are overloaded with choices, but they lack clarity. The number of available options distracts us from the focus we need to succeed.

I believe what you need to succeed in your real estate business is a CLEAR PLAN that is well crafted around YOUR UNIQUE STRENGTHS.[1] Once you have that plan, if you stay CONSISTENT to the point of MASTERY, you will find success in this business. And once you have that, the sky's the limit.

Too many agents fall prey to the shiny object syndrome.

---

1 See "Discover your power," chapter 27.

They try something for a month. It doesn't work. Then they see something that looks better. So they abandon the first strategy in favor of the next one. But they don't stick with that one long enough to make it work either. So they move on to the next shiny object.

That's a recipe for failure. But it's so easy to be infected by this syndrome. Walk into any company business meeting, and ideas are floating everywhere. Podcasts, YouTube videos, seminars, webinars, and the list of the latest and greatest ways to improve your business goes on and on. Most agents jump from idea to idea, lose focus, and run like crazy on the hamster wheel.

In this book, you will receive the guidance you need to bring clarity to your business—not someone else's. I will show you how to build your own plan—custom designed for you according to your unique strengths.

In addition to information overload and lack of focus, most real estate agents who don't make it in this business lack confidence in themselves. I want to help you gain (or restore) the confidence you need. Confidence is like a muscle. If you exercise it, it will grow stronger. I will show you how.

I hope this book is a game changer for you!

Neil Mathweg

Summer 2021

Part One: Mary's Story

1. Trapped!

It had been a long day. The parking lot was nearly empty when Mary collapsed into her sun-baked car. The project at her corporate job was sucking the life out of her. But if she didn't pull something off at work, she and her entire team were going to be laid off.

Adding to the stress: Mary's son came home sick from school. But because of everything going on at the office, there was no way Mary could go home early to be with him. She was heartbroken that she couldn't be there to hold her son.

To make things even worse, she was in the middle of a stint of the silent treatment with her husband, John. The night prior, Mary broke down to him about the stress at work, and about her dream to get out of the corporate world and become a real estate agent. The conversation didn't end well. John tried to understand Mary's dream, but fear of not having a steady paycheck coming in was something John couldn't wrap his head around. Mary tried to convince him that they could use their savings so Mary could make the transition. It would just be a few months and then the money will start coming in. That scared John to the point it made it look like he didn't believe in her, which then spiraled into a huge fight.

Trapped.

She felt so trapped. She hated her job, couldn't be there for her kids, and on top of that, she felt like her husband didn't believe in her. The only thing that made her happy or made her feel some hope was thinking about becoming a real estate agent.

Ever since Mary and her husband bought their first home two years earlier, she dreamed of becoming a real estate agent. During the process of buying their home, Mary noticed a few things about their agent: She drove a brand new BMW, lived in a custom-built home, and had people working for her. She was a boss… a mom boss. She had it together, and she seemed so happy. There was something else Mary saw—freedom!

After a good cry in the parking lot, Mary saw her boss walking out of the building toward her. Mary quickly put on her sunglasses and shifted the car into drive. Mary looked up as her boss was passing by. Mary smiled and waved, but her boss barely acknowledged her. Her curt head nod was so cold it only added more hurt.

All Mary could think about on the way home was *How do I get out of this?* She cried on and off the entire ride home. She couldn't take another day at this job.

That night at home, John attempted to apologize.

"I didn't mean to hurt you," he said. "I didn't mean to say I don't believe in you. I just didn't think you were being reasonable—using our savings to chase this dream. And I don't think being a real estate agent is all that it is cracked up to be."

"Yes, John," she replied, "But this is my dream—not yours."

While getting ready the next morning, Mary got an email from her boss. The email was sent to her entire team. It read:

> Mandatory meeting this morning at 9:00 in the large conference room.

Nothing more, nothing less.

All Mary could think about was that they were going to pile on even more stress in working on the project. Her anxiety began to set in.

She arrived at the office and walked straight to the conference room. She noticed things were a little off. Her boss walked in shortly after 9:00 with a very sad look on her face. She sat down and began to explain that everyone on the team was being laid off. "The company has decided to go in another direction and the lay off is effective immediately. Everyone needs to clear out their desks, turn in their laptops, and be out of the building by noon," she said. Each person would receive pay for three months, and health insurance for the remainder of the year.

Suddenly Mary's boss's behavior from the day before made sense. No wonder she didn't wave. No wonder she didn't smile. She knew the bad news she needed to deliver in the morning.

Looking around the room, Mary saw looks of devastation on every face. But inside she was smiling. *What a relief!*

Of course she felt some trepidation, some fear of the unknown. But that was more than offset by her excitement. The way was clear for her to become what she wanted to be: a real estate agent. And she also felt relief because her new plans didn't require her boss's approval. For the first-time in her life, she was on her own!

When she got back to her desk, she texted John to give him the news.

"Oh, no!" was his reply. "Now what are we going to do?"

To Mary, the answer was obvious. "I'm going into real estate."

She went home that day trying to contain her excitement. She knew the layoff would be a problem for John. He would be scared, looking at the risk, but she was excited, looking at the possibilities.

Before everyone got home from school and from work, Mary had done all of the research. She only had three months to get sales going before they needed to dip into their savings. She needed to get her license and go on a fast track. She had the entire plan worked out and ready to present to John when he got home.

When John got home that night, it went great. John was nervous, no doubt, but also agreed that now was the best time to give it a shot. They also agreed that Mary would get a part-time job waiting tables at John's sister's restaurant a few nights a week. It was a job Mary did while she was in college, and she knew she could pick up right where she left off.

2. Early signs of success

For the next three weeks Mary studied nonstop preparing to take her test, and, hopefully, get her license.

To take a break from studying, Mary reconnected with the agent who helped them buy their house. They met for coffee and it went great. She welcomed Mary with open arms, inviting her to join their company, and said she would do everything she could to help her grow her business. She explained her company offered in-office training and a coaching program Mary could jump into once she had her license.

The conversation couldn't have gone any better, and it felt like a confirmation that going into real estate was the right choice for her. Everything was coming together.

Mary also announced on Facebook that she was laid off, and had decided to become a real estate agent. She was so excited to pass her test because she couldn't wait to tell everyone she had officially become an agent.

With the amount of people she knew, she expected people to come flocking to her once she announced she was an agent. The signs were already there. The first post she put out there to let people know of her upcoming career change just blew up. She hadn't had so many likes and comments since the birth of their son. On top of that, with all of the people she knew from her corporate job, plus waiting tables for so many years, she would have all the business she needed.

Mary couldn't wait to get that license in her hands.

3. Passed!

Mary needed to be to the state licensing building by 8:30 am. She could hardly sleep because she was so excited. This was the moment she was waiting for. Today was the day! She was going to become a real estate agent!

She got there on time, coffee in hand, makeup and hair on point for that selfie she was going to be taking later with the license in hand. You know—all the essentials ready to go.

Three hours later she was finished. She hit "submit" and watched the spinning wheel. Did she pass? Was she going to get her license?

YES!

She did it! She had become a real estate agent!

She immediately called her husband to share the excitement. "I did it! I'm officially a real estate agent!"

John caught some of the elation and even offered to take her to lunch to celebrate.

To top it off, the selfie came out perfect, and now her phone was blowing up with people congratulating her. It was such a good day—the day she had been dreaming of for a long time.

At the end of the day, she settled into bed and turned off the lamp with a smile on her face. She couldn't be happier.

4. 87% don't make it!

In the two months that followed getting her license, Mary attended one training after another. She wanted to connect with her friend in the office, but that didn't happen. The other agent was too busy. So instead of in-depth insider advice from her friend, she got this cryptic text: "Fake it till you make it."

Not much help.

So far, it was not coming together. Three months of severance pay was about to end. And, yes, Mary was waitressing to pick up extra money, but that barely covered all the expenses involved in becoming an agent. John was starting to freak out.

Money. She needed to get money coming in. Until she did, she was stuck. There was no way she could tell John that the money wasn't there. She didn't have an accepted offer. A couple of buyers were looking, but that was it.

Sure. The office had a coaching program. Mary could sum it up in one sentence:

Make 50 to 100 calls a day to FSBOs and Expireds.

She looked at her phone trying to summon the willpower to make another pointless phone call to someone who would probably hang up on her.

I don't know what I was thinking, but this wasn't it.

Mary didn't know which she feared more—the constant rejection, or the possibility that one of these FSBOs might actually ask for a listing appointment. *Then what would I do?* she wondered. *I wouldn't choose a rookie like me over an experienced agent. How could I talk someone into doing something that I wouldn't even do myself?*

As the office manager walked by her desk, he probably saw the defeated look on her face, because he stopped to give her one of his "go-team-go" pep talks. "Just make the calls. You can do it! It will work for you!"

She worked up a smile, but inside she was thinking: *How can I tell you this isn't working? Your pep talk feels cheap. It feels fake. You're making me feel like a sleazy used car salesperson. It isn't me. And it isn't working.*

Open houses. One of the top agents in the office told her to host open houses. "That's where the buyers are," she said, "It's a great way to build your business."

That sounded fantastic. Mary started hosting open houses for other agents in her office every weekend. After four weeks of this, her enthusiasm started to wane. Yes, she met buyers (along with tire kickers), but those meetings didn't take her where she wanted to go. "Sorry," they said, "we're already working with an agent. Sorry." Oh, yes, there was one exception: A young couple did give Mary their names and a phone number. The next morning she called.

The phone was disconnected.

I don't know what it takes to reel people in from open houses, she said to herself, *but it's pretty clear I don't have it.*

But there's always friends, right?

At first, Mary thought for sure she would get her first clients from her group of friends. So she started calling through the list.

"Oh, yeah, Mary, we'd love to." *When we're ready to buy. When we're ready to sell. When the time is right. Sometime in the future. Maybe twenty years from now. Maybe a hundred years from now.*

Nobody was ready now, and Mary needed a now, not a maybe, not a someday, but a now.

"Couldn't you just sell your home now?" she felt like asking. But she didn't. The last thing she wanted to do was drive her friends away by coming across like a pushy sales person.

As Mary phoned through her list of friends, a nagging voice in the back of her mind started to chant her deepest fear:

What if you say yes? Then what will I do? What if I blow it? What if I don't do a good job? What if I disappoint you, and I mess up everything for you? Other agents in my office negotiate sweet deals for their clients. How do they do it? I have no idea. I'm clueless.

So much for those Facebook posts with all those likes and "congratulations."

Mary's office manager had been giving her internet leads to work. Great, right? No. Another dead end. She couldn't get anyone to call her back. She kept leaving messages like everyone said to do. She even tried texting them. After seventy-five calls, she racked up two responses:

1. "Not interested."

2. "Stop! Take me off your list now!"

No wonder 87% of agents don't make it past five years! I don't know how they even make it past a year!

Mary was running out of time and running out of ideas.

There's gotta be a better way...

While sitting at her cubicle Mary Googled, "How to make it as a new real estate agent."

Among the results, she found a podcast that looked promising.

Hmm... Something to listen to on the way home.

5. Shiny object syndrome

Mary turned on the podcast and eased her car out of the parking lot. Neil, the host, started out by telling her what she already knew: It's hard to make it as a new agent. Really hard.

"No lie," Mary said aloud.

"But what makes new agents fail?" the host asked. "Two things: First, the shiny object syndrome, and second, lack of congruency. Let me explain…"

Agents try one thing one day and another thing the next. They chase the next shiny object, the idea that seems good, but they don't stay consistent with anything long enough to succeed.

And why do they get stuck in the "shiny object syndrome"? Because they don't have a clear plan that's congruent with them—a plan that fits their personality.

Wow! Mary thought about how much she hated every minute of calling those FSBOs and Expireds. *Open houses aren't working. Those internet leads are impossible.*

Her plan, if she had one, definitely wasn't congruent with her personality. And, even if it was, it wasn't working.

Neil went on to discuss something he called the "Three

Pillar Plan." He explained how it was possible to create a Three Pillar Plan™ that fit your unique personality—a plan that would work and would empower you to build a successful real estate business.

That sounded magical to Mary. *Where was this guy three months ago?!*

Mary kept listening, and then, instead of turning into her driveway, took a ride around her side of the city just to listen to another episode.

Everything Neil was saying made sense. Spot on. As his podcast came to a close, he said, "If you need to talk, just reach out to me."

Absolutely, Mary thought. *You're gonna get a call from me.*

When Mary looked up Neil's contact information later that evening, she was surprised to discover that she and he lived in the same city, Madison, Wisconsin.

Wow!

Mary sat down to her keyboard and started typing: "I have been listening to your podcast. It has been so good! I was wondering if you could help me. I am a few months in, and I am struggling to put my first deal together. I have a few things going, but nothing is certain. I'm not sure I can afford your coaching but at this point I don't have anywhere else to turn." And then, just before hitting send, she added, "Wow! We're both in Madison. How cool is that?"

Neil's reply came the next morning:

"I'd be happy to help any way I can. Since we're both in Madison, let's grab coffee. Just go to my website www.agentrisecoaching.com and schedule a time with me."

That was easy! Maybe I can finally get the help I need...

6. A business you love

When Mary arrived at the coffee shop to meet with Neil, her nerves were jangling. There was so much to cover, and so much riding on this meeting!

After a bit of small talk, Neil asked, "What do you love about this business?"

Mary searched for words. She had been so excited to get into real estate. But the dream had almost turned into a nightmare. Nothing was what she expected. Nothing was working the way she wanted it to. She didn't want to sound negative, but what would she gain by lying?

She took a deep breath and plunged in. "I can't say I love much. I have been instructed to 'dial for dollars' and I hate every second of it. I feel like a robot that is broken. I don't like being salesy, and I feel like I can't be who I am and be successful at the same time."

Neil nodded. "Believe me, I get it. Your situation is very common. Before you were told to call FSBOs and Expireds, how did you dream you were going to build the business?"

"To be honest with you, I thought friends and family would just call on me. I also thought open houses would be a great way to find clients. But none of that is working."

"You need to know: you're not alone here. This happens to many new agents. But let's zero in on family and friends—your sphere of influence. What have you done to reach them?"

"I posted on Facebook and Instagram that I'm an agent. I called friends on my contact list," Mary said.

"Okay, that's great. But nothing more? Have you mailed anything?

"No, that's it."

Neil made a note on his tablet. "Okay, I understand. Earlier you said you have tried open houses but haven't had success. What else have you done?"

Mary sighed just thinking about it. "Well, my broker has given me some online leads to go after, but I can't get any of them to call me back."

"Got it. So, Mary, out of all the things you've tried—putting results aside for a moment—what do you like most?"

That was an unexpected question. "Wow," Mary said, "I've never been asked what I like most. Instead, it's always been: Do this or you won't be successful."

"I hear that all the time from clients. But here's the dirty little secret: It isn't true."

"So," Mary asked, "are you saying I can actually do things that I like and still be successful?"

Neil laughed, and his laugh was infectious. "Yes, that's

exactly what I'm saying." Then he added, "Here's the thing: We want to build a business you love, and if you are doing a bunch of things you hate, you'll never stay consistent. Success comes from staying consistent."

After thinking for a moment, Mary said, "I would love to work with people I know. I hate calling online leads, FSBOs and Expireds. I feel like I'm chasing them and begging for their business. It feels salesy, and I hate that. I also really like doing open houses because you can meet people face-to-face, get to know them, and then start working with them. Too bad it doesn't work."

Neil laughed again. "Wait a second! You find what you love to do. I'll show you how to make it work."

"Really?" Mary could hardly believe what she was hearing.

"Really."

Neil paused to take a long sip of coffee. Then he continued: "You can build the business you love. But not the way you're currently operating. You have a bad case of 'shiny object syndrome.' You try something for a while. It doesn't work. So you chase the next shiny object that comes along, hoping to find what works for you. But that's not how real estate works. You can find a strategy that works for you, but you gotta do it right, and you gotta stay consistent. Do it right. Stay consistent. You need both. When you have both, you will succeed."

Now Mary was starting to take notes.

"You need to know: you're not alone here. This happens to many new agents. But let's zero in on family and friends—your sphere of influence. What have you done to reach them?"

"I posted on Facebook and Instagram that I'm an agent. I called friends on my contact list," Mary said.

"Okay, that's great. But nothing more? Have you mailed anything?

"No, that's it."

Neil made a note on his tablet. "Okay, I understand. Earlier you said you have tried open houses but haven't had success. What else have you done?"

Mary sighed just thinking about it. "Well, my broker has given me some online leads to go after, but I can't get any of them to call me back."

"Got it. So, Mary, out of all the things you've tried—putting results aside for a moment—what do you like most?"

That was an unexpected question. "Wow," Mary said, "I've never been asked what I like most. Instead, it's always been: Do this or you won't be successful."

"I hear that all the time from clients. But here's the dirty little secret: It isn't true."

"So," Mary asked, "are you saying I can actually do things that I like and still be successful?"

Neil laughed, and his laugh was infectious. "Yes, that's

exactly what I'm saying." Then he added, "Here's the thing: We want to build a business you love, and if you are doing a bunch of things you hate, you'll never stay consistent. Success comes from staying consistent."

After thinking for a moment, Mary said, "I would love to work with people I know. I hate calling online leads, FSBOs and Expireds. I feel like I'm chasing them and begging for their business. It feels salesy, and I hate that. I also really like doing open houses because you can meet people face-to-face, get to know them, and then start working with them. Too bad it doesn't work."

Neil laughed again. "Wait a second! You find what you love to do. I'll show you how to make it work."

"Really?" Mary could hardly believe what she was hearing.

"Really."

Neil paused to take a long sip of coffee. Then he continued: "You can build the business you love. But not the way you're currently operating. You have a bad case of 'shiny object syndrome.' You try something for a while. It doesn't work. So you chase the next shiny object that comes along, hoping to find what works for you. But that's not how real estate works. You can find a strategy that works for you, but you gotta do it right, and you gotta stay consistent. Do it right. Stay consistent. You need both. When you have both, you will succeed."

Now Mary was starting to take notes.

Neil continued, "We want to build your business with a clear plan so you know what to do every single day. We want that plan to be congruent to you. It needs to feel right. It needs to work for you. It needs to be something you're excited about doing, something that fits your personality. Then we want you to stay consistent with that plan."

"That would be great!"

Neil handed Mary a piece of paper with a diagram on it. "The key to your real estate success will be found in something we call the Three Pillar Plan™."[2]

[See next page…]

Neil pointed to the top section of the diagram. "The first pillar is your Sphere of Influence. With this pillar we want to mail something to each person in your sphere each and every month. We want them to know you take this business seriously, we want them to know you are a successful agent, and lastly we want to know others are referring to you and therefore they should refer to you too.

"Your sphere of influence eventually will make up 80% or more of your business. But if they never hear from you, then they won't take action. You have to remember that just because they know you doesn't mean that they will call on you. They probably know another agent, if not five other agents. How are you going to stand out as their go-to? This consistent monthly mailing is going to show that you are in

---

[2] Get your copy of the Three Pillar Plan™ at agentrisecoaching.com/resources.

this business for real. You are here for them and others are trusting you too.

AGENT RISE THREE PILLAR PLAN™

01 SPHERE OF INFLUENCE PILLAR™

DETAILS

- ☐ **Option 1:** Newsletter Subscription
- ☐ **Option 2:** My Own Newsletter
- ☐ **Option 3:** Letter of the Heart
- ☐ **Option 4:** Other _____

02 CHASE PILLAR™

DETAILS

- ☐ **Option 1:** Open Houses w/ MatchMaker
- ☐ **Option 2:** Facebook Ads w/ MatchMaker
- ☐ **Option 3:** Online Leads w/ MatchMaker
- ☐ **Option 4:** Expired and FSBO hunting
- ☐ **Option 5:** Geo Farming
- ☐ **Option 6:** Niche _____

03 ATTRACTION PILLAR™

DETAILS

- ☐ **Option 1:** YouTube Channel Focused
- ☐ **Option 2:** Niche Social Media Ecosystem
- ☐ **Option 3:** Social Agent Plan
- ☐ **Option 4:** One Platform Focused (Instagram, LinkedIn)
- ☐ **Option 5:** Podcasting with Social Agent Plan
- ☐ **Option 6:** Other Blogging with Social Agent Plan
- ☐ **Option 7:** Other _____

AGENT RISE   agentrisecoaching.com

"But you can't ask someone to trust you, you have to earn their trust. Sending a monthly mailing helps you earn their trust. It shows you are consistent. The consistency piece is what pays off and helps you build that trust."

Mary looked up from her notes. "I have to confess, I'm a little embarrassed. I don't know how I could have thought a couple posts on Facebook and a few phone calls would get clients knocking at my door. Compared to what you're describing here, I haven't reached out to my friends and family at all."

Neil smiled. "It's a mistake most beginners make. But now you know, and that puts you way ahead of your competition."

Now it was Mary's turn to smile. Neil continued, "However, we're not going to stop with just one pillar. Just as a chair or a stool with only one leg is going to fall over, so also a business plan with only one pillar is not stable. We call our second pillar the Chase pillar. The purpose of the Chase Pillar™ is to connect you with clients you can't reach through your Sphere of Influence. It allows you to meet new people.

"Of the different options available in the Chase Pillar™, I think you are meant to do open houses. It fits your personality so well because you are outgoing, and you like to work with people you know. With open houses you get a face-to-face opportunity to connect with people right from the beginning. You don't get that with some other options like online leads. Plus, I just see you mixing in with people so well."

Mary shook her head. "I'm not so sure. I tried open

houses. I couldn't get them to work."

"Everything works," Neil said, and then he held up a hand as Mary was about to object. "Everything works; you just need to learn to do it the right way."

"Okay. Yes. I'm sorry. I need to get that in my head."

"No worries," Neil said. "I'll show you how to work open houses the right way[3] so that you actually get leads from them. Right now you are doing open houses just like every other agent. You are looking for this special moment with the buyer where you feel like you just became best friends with them. It's magical. You hit it off, set up a coffee date to talk real estate, and you whisk them away to go help them buy a house. Sound familiar?"

Mary laughed. "Yeah, that sounds about right."

"Well, the truth is that is a very rare thing. It's kind of the unicorn opportunity. When we get to working on your Chase Pillar™ I'll teach you a more dialed in way to actually extract leads from the open house no matter how much you hit it off with the buyer. It's a game changer. If you do it right, open houses can help you build a very successful business."

"Wow," Mary said. "This is making so much sense. I was doing things that weren't right for me—they didn't fit my personality, so I hated doing them. Not only that, it sounds like I was doing them the wrong way. On top of that, I

---

[3] In Chapter 13, "Chase Pillar™ & lead generation," we'll explain the right way to do open houses.

wasn't even being consistent."

"The nice thing about all of that is this: We can solve those problems. But let me take a moment to talk about the third and final pillar—the Attraction pillar."

"Attraction… Does that mean we use social media?"

"Yes, but with a purpose. We need to do social media with a purpose. Social media is great, but it's a very noisy place, and we need to give our followers direction. We need to post with a purpose. We do that through certain niches and certain platforms, and then we build an ecosystem around the niche. We then drive traffic to the content through organic search—free—and ads—paid. We do this with a great lead generation magnet and follow-up system. We'll talk all about this when we get to building your Attraction pillar."

Mary's mind was in overdrive. "Okay, this is fantastic," she said, "but what do I work on first. How do I build this out?"

"Great question. This is where the Agent Rise Steps™ come into play. Let me explain: Most agents do things out of order. They see a top producing agent with a logo and brand, fancy cards, a great looking website, huge social media presence and swag, and imagine that this is how the top producing agent became successful. But do you want to know the truth?"

Mary nodded.

"The logo, the business cards, the swag—all of this had very little to do with their success. Let me put it this way. When your transmission is broken, do you hire someone to wax your car? No! It doesn't matter how great the car looks if it doesn't run, right? Same thing with your business. We need to make sure it's running great before we start making it look great. So with that in mind let me show you the steps we'll take to build out your business."

[See next page...][4]

Mary looked it over and said, "I need to say my mind is officially blown! I never thought this much clarity was even possible. I've learned more here, in one hour, than I have in the last three months.

"Look, I don't know how I'm going to afford to hire you as a coach, but I also know I can't afford NOT to hire you. Let me go home and talk this over with my husband."

---

4   Also available at agentrisecoaching.com/resources.

AGENT RISE STEPS™

01 **Create Database**
Start with 100 people you know to identify your Sphere of Influence Pillar™ (SOI)

02 **Announce Yourself**
Mail out announcement letter to your SOI

03 **Know Your Sphere of Influence**
Select and mantain your SOI Pillar™

04 **Chase Business**
Select and maintain your Chase Pillar™

05 **Convert Leads**
Set up your MatchMaker System™

06 **Systematize**
Create repeatable processes in your business

07 **Attract Business**
Select and maintain your Attraction Pillar™

08 **Grow Your Sphere of Influence**
It's time to take your SOI to the next level...
It's time for Sphere of Influence 2.0 by adding more people

AGENT RISE

agentrisecoaching.com

8. Your identity

Of course John was afraid of spending the money. But Mary knew they had no other choice. This was the only way her real estate business was going to get off the ground.

Mary woke up super excited to get started with coaching. The first thing Neil had her do was to begin building a database of around 100 people. At first this sounded simple, but when working on it a lot of fear began to bubble up.

As Mary looked through the names in front of her, these thoughts started rolling around in her mind. *Ouch! I haven't stayed in touch with these people as much as I should have. Now I'm gonna mail them letters and say, "Look at me! I'm a real estate agent just like five other people you know. Come buy a house with me." Awkward!*

When Mary arrived at the session, she told Neil she was struggling to put together the list of 100 names. She expected him to brush it off and say something like, "Just do it!"

But instead Neil said, "This is a limiting belief. When we care too much about what people think of us, we allow others to determine our identity. This is the disease to please. It stems from a fear of rejection, but that fear can be cured by knowing your identity."

Wow! Mary wasn't expecting that. But as she pondered what he was saying, she realized he was 100% right.

"Neil, you're right," she said. "For the longest time I've had this fear of what other people are thinking about me."

"Can you tell me more?"

"I'm really concerned with how I'm coming across. With these mailings, for example, I'm afraid of people thinking I'm too salesy. When looking at the names and addresses all I think about is; what are they going to think when they get my mail?"

"I understand," Neil said. Many people have this fear. But here's the truth: You can't let anyone else determine your identity. You are a child of God, and it really doesn't matter what anyone else thinks of you. And that does not come off as an arrogant statement, rather one of confidence in knowing your identity."

"I guess, to be honest, I really wonder why they would go with me rather than with some other more experienced agent they already know."

"I get that. A lot of new agents feel that way. But I'll show you how to get around that.[5] Meanwhile, here's an-

---

5   People crave trust from their agent. In fact, NAR reports that consumers would rather trust their agent than know that their agent has a ton of experience. This is music to a new agent's ears. You must earn peoples trust, be honest with them, explain exactly where you are, and ask for an opportunity. More on this in a few pages.

other truth: These people who receive your letters are not your provider. God is. So when you feel the disease to please come creeping up, simply remind yourself: 'God is my provider.'"

"Wow! I never ever thought of looking at it that way. That is so powerful."

"It's something that takes time to settle in. When I first learned this, it took me a few months before I really believed it. Now today, any bit of anxiety that creeps in can be pushed out by reminding myself who my provider is. A deal that is going rough, I say 'I'm the son of the Living King, and that will never be taken away from me. No one else is my provider. God is my provider—always has been and always will be."

"So you just say that and the anxiety leaves?"

"Yep," Neil said. "It's the truth, and the truth will set you free. When I first learned this truth, it came at a time where I was so wrapped up in what people thought of me. I was consumed by five star reviews and words of affirmation. I was devastated when someone I knew listed their house with another agent. I was constantly worried about who hired me and if they were 100% satisfied with my services. All of this is good in the sense of providing great service, but it's horrible for our mindsets. We become slaves to others and we lack any identity in who we are. It was a sad place to be, and it didn't allow me to be who I was meant to be. I would lose sleep at night worried about getting someone's approval. I had so much fear of being rejected by someone that I couldn't hardly stand it. In fact, there were times when I would ruin my entire day because I was afraid someone was rejecting me."

"Wow, Neil! This is so much bigger than just getting the strength to mail a letter. I can see this changing everything."

"Exactly! This will carry you to new heights. Agents who break through do so because their confidence increases and their disease to please decreases. They walk in confidence knowing who their provider is, and they won't let anyone else determine otherwise. They won't let anyone rob them of their joy in living life."

9. Your announcement Letter

Over the next couple of weeks, Mary worked with Neil to overcome her "disease to please." Not only did this empower her to complete her database, but it also gave her a whole new outlook on life. Understanding her identity as a daughter of God gave her new confidence—confidence that will never be taken from her.

When her database was complete, she was ready to send her first mailing to friends and family. But she was stuck. *What should the letter say?*

"I need help figuring out how to write this," she said to Neil.

"No problem. Your letter needs to include three elements. First, it needs to resonate with your reader. In other words, it can't be solely about you. Your reader needs to feel your letter pertains to them. Second, you need to ask for the opportunity to serve them. Do NOT 'fake it till you make it. Don't act like you're perfect. Be honest, and ask for the opportunity. Third, you need an easy call-to-action— NOT one that says, 'Call me if you're thinking of buying or selling.'"

"Can you break that down for me a little bit?"

"Sure. As far as resonating with your reader goes, we

need to state the obvious. In other words, we announce that you are a new real estate agent ... and the truth is: your reader probably knows another agent—if not five other agents. When you acknowledge that, your reader will continue reading because they stand in an agreement with you."

"Okay," Mary said, "but I don't know how much I want to emphasize how little experience I have. If the letter comes across as: Look at me; I'm a brand new real estate agent, won't that turn people away?"

"What would you do instead?"

"I don't know. Don't I want to come across as confident? Don't I want to let people know I have a team behind me, and that I'm ready to take on any client, any challenge?"

Neil smiled. "In other words, fake it till you make it?"

"Hmm. Maybe?"

Neil shook his head. "No. You don't want to do that. Absolutely not. And let me tell you why. Honesty is your best friend. Always. Especially when you're new. People see right through 'fake it till you make it.' And they don't appreciate it. Instead, they want you to be honest with them, to tell them exactly where you are at, and to ask them for an opportunity."

"I don't want to be dishonest."

"No. Of course you don't. And here's why: We're building trust. Trust requires honesty. Your clients need to be able to trust you completely. If you fake it, if you fudge, if you bend the truth, then trust goes out the window. But there's another reason why you want to be upfront about being new."

"What's that?"

"When you go to a restaurant and your waiter is brand new, don't you find yourself supporting and encouraging them as they learn their job?"

"Yeah, I guess I do."

"When they're new, mistakes are allowed and acceptable. You might even find yourself giving them a larger tip just to show them: 'You've got this!'"

"Same way in real estate?"

"Yes. The same is true in real estate. If you're new and admit it, people by nature will support and encourage you ... but only if you're honest and upfront about it. People want to give you an opportunity—if you ask for it."

Neil took another sip of coffee before continuing. "Let me tell you a story. A number of years ago, someone came to me looking to purchase a home on the lake. He was looking for property in the one to three million dollar range. That was way beyond my experience at the time. In those days, my median deal was a $250,000 home, and my biggest deal was a $600,000 property.

"Anyway, my prospective client asked a few general questions, and then he got straight to the point: 'Why should I pick you to be my agent?'

"I had to be honest. I said to him, 'I know you are looking for a lakefront specialist, and that is not me. In fact I have never even sold a house on the lake. I'm a minivan driving dad from Sun Prairie, who lost his shorts in the recession, didn't file bankruptcy, and I'm paying off all that debt to get my family out of the hole I got us in. Representing you will be the largest deal of my career, and I won't take that lightly. I will work my tail off to assure you get the best house for the best price in the best area. I would be honored if you gave me the opportunity to serve you.'

"There was a pause on the other end of the phone, and then he said, 'I want you to be my real estate agent!'

"When we got to the closing, I asked him, 'Why did you go with me.' He said, 'Because you were honest in representing who you are. You didn't fluff anything. I figured if you could be honest in explaining your good AND your bad, then you would be honest in representing me.'

"He also went on to say everyone else he met with talked about how great they were. They sent him flashy brochures in the mail in an attempt to impress him. Me—I did none of that. I just told the truth. Then he laughed. 'I'll never forget the line,' he said, '"I'm a minivan driving dad."'

"Do you see what I'm saying about faking it until you make it? Don't do it. Be honest and ask for an opportunity."

"Wow!" Mary said. "This makes so much sense. I think I'm starting to figure out what needs to go into this first letter."[6]

Mary left the meeting filled with a sense of confidence. Yes, she was a new agent, but it's okay to be new. She didn't need to fake it till she made it. That was liberating. She could be who she was.

Later, as she was listening to one of Neil's podcasts, she heard him say, "Confidence is a muscle." *It is,* she told herself. *It is a muscle. And I can already feel myself getting stronger.*

---

[6] Want to write the perfect announcement letter? Agent Rise members have access to this and many templates inside Agent Rise Coaching. Go to agentrisecoaching.com to learn more.

10. Sphere of Influence Pillar™

The next week Mary started working with a first-time buyer. *This is really fun!* she thought. She felt like she was really good at working with them. She also felt fully alive when working with them.

Hmm. Maybe I should just focus on working with first-time home buyers. Some agents choose a niche. Maybe mine should be first-time home buyers.

"What do you think?" Mary asked Neil at their next meeting. "After all, it's been so much fun working with this first-time buyer. I've been able to explain the buying process to her, guide her in the right direction—there hasn't been a single question she's asked that I haven't been able to answer. I'm loving it!"

"That is fantastic," Neil said, "but let me tell you a little secret: It's not working with first-time buyers you are loving. No. Instead, it is your growth in confidence you're loving. Over time, you'll get that same growth in confidence with experienced buyers, sellers, investors, and more. You are growing!"

"I never thought of it like that. So maybe I shouldn't pick first-time buyers as my niche?"

"I wouldn't, no. Don't stop with first-time buyers. You'll

want to represent more than first-time buyers. As you get more experience, you'll discover that first-time buyers are usually more work than experienced buyers. On top of that, when you work with a first-time buyer, you only get one side of a transaction. But if you work with a move up or move down buyer, you can get up to three sides—the house they are buying, the house they are selling, and possibly the buying side of the house they are selling. You also get connected with buyers who don't buy your client's house, but might work with you to buy a different house. It opens the door to many possibilities.

"So, no, don't pigeon hole yourself as a first-time home buyer specialist. If you do, then when the first-time buyer you worked with wants to sell her house, she won't call you because you can't help her—you don't work with sellers, you specialize in first-time buyers."

Mary set her cup of coffee down on the table. "I think you just saved me from making a huge mistake. It's not about first-time home buyers. It's about growing in confidence, and trusting yourself enough to step out of your comfort zone. Thank you!"

Then they got back to the task at hand for that meeting: going over Mary's announcement letter and getting that ready to mail. Mary nailed all three essentials in the draft she showed Neil, so the letter was a go.

"I'll get this in the mail this week, and I guess that starts the clock for the newsletter I'll be sending out."

"Fantastic!" Neil said.

"But I have a question. Of course I will mail out this first announcement letter. But after that, is it really necessary to mail my newsletter? Wouldn't it make more sense to email it?"

"I'm not gonna knock emailing," Neil said. "It's free. You gotta like free. However, you get what you pay for. The open rate for email is 30%. At best. If you're lucky. Usually it's less. We don't know the exact open rate with mail, but I guarantee it's higher than 30%. With email, people can and do unsubscribe. With snail mail, people know you are making an investment to reach them. They respect that."

Mary nodded. "Okay, that makes sense. More expensive. But much better."

"That's right. Email has its place. And we will return to email later. In Agent Rise Step 8 or Sphere of Influence 2.0, we can add email.

"Meanwhile, keep in mind that consistency is the most important part of mailing a newsletter. You want to demonstrate to your sphere of influence that you take this seriously. You also want to consistently show your family and friends that people are referring clients to you. In the newsletter, you'll feature a gratitude section where you thank those who have recently referred you."

"Okay," Mary said. "Sending a monthly newsletter makes sense to me. But I do have a question. What if I get writer's block? I mean, I don't know if I can come up with something new to say every month."

"I hear you," Neil said. "But there's an easy solution to that. Subscribe to a newsletter service. The service writes all the articles for you. You get an email once a month with all of their material. Then you add or remove whatever you want to make the newsletter your own. If you're really swamped on a given month, just send it out as is. If you have more time, then you can spend more time customizing it. This way you stay consistent."

"Because consistency is the most important aspect of mailing newsletters," Mary chimed in.

"Right."

"But why?"

"The main reason for consistently mailing out a newsletter every month is to show your people that you take your business seriously. You show them month after month, year after year, you are here for them. There was a time in my career where I stepped out of sales to lead a firm. In this move, I stopped mailing to my database. It was one of the worst mistakes I ever made in my career. The year prior I had done around 60 transactions from my sphere of influence. The year after the move, I referred 35 transactions to agents in my firm from my sphere, the next year 14, and then down to 5! See how that dwindled away. If you miss just one month, your friends and family—your sphere of influence see you are slacking. They think, *If she doesn't take sending out her newsletter seriously, then does she even take her business seriously?* These are the questions they will ask themselves, and we don't want to give them the opportunity to entertain these kinds of thoughts."

"Okay. Wow! That makes sense. I can see how consistently mailing a newsletter will help. But will it be enough? Will it get me the clients I need?"

"Great question. And here's the answer: no. By itself, no. But you need it. Later on, when we get to Step 8 of the Agent Rise program, I'll show you what to do in addition to the newsletter so that you can gain the clients you need through your sphere of influence. For now, mailing your newsletter shows your people that you are in this business to stay. You are going to show them consistency. Your monthly newsletter will be the foundation that we'll build on as we grow your business.

"By sending a monthly newsletter, you can expect to get calls from about 10% of the people in your sphere per year. If you have 150 people in your database, that could mean 15 sales a year just from your sphere of influence. When we get to Step 8, I'll show you how to double your results with add-on methods to connect with your sphere."

"Add on methods?"

"Sure. We'll get into it in detail later,[7] but they could include client events, gift drop offs, VIP programs, and/or email campaigns."

---

7   See Chapter 20, "Sphere of Influence 2.0."

11. Compete against yourself

Mary left her meeting with Neil fired up. She could feel her confidence soaring.

But then it all came crashing down.

Here's how it happened. She went to her company's monthly business meeting ready to get fired up and gain even more confidence. But then her broker started giving shout outs to agents who were flourishing. One of those agents started a full month after Mary did, and already had two closings. On top of that, she had a new listing and was working with four other buyers. Then the broker singled out another agent. He just celebrated the completion of his first year with his seventeenth closing.

17!

Mary sat in the back corner of the room and wanted to disappear. In her four months with the company, Mary had not had a single closing. Not even one.

As she felt tears forming in her eyes, she slipped out of the meeting and made her way down the hall into the women's room. There she looked at herself in the mirror.

I feel like a loser. Am I even in the right business. Am I really cut out to be a real estate agent?

For the rest of the day, she struggled to even function. She tried to get a newsletter out, but her heart wasn't in it. Time slowly ticked by. When mid-afternoon finally arrived, she grabbed her jacket and headed for the parking lot. All she really wanted to do was crawl back into bed.

A few days later when she met with Neil, she told him the whole story. "I left our last session feeling completely fired up. Now, I feel like all of that has been punched right out of me. I'm hurt. I'm angry at our broker. I'm angry at my colleagues. But I'm mostly angry at myself. Who am I trying to fool? I don't know if I can even do this. I feel like quitting."

Neil nodded and smiled. Then he said, "This is great!"

"What! How can you say, 'This is great!'?"

"Because..." Neil said, "...you are about to experience another breakthrough."

"What do you mean? How?"

"Here's the thing. You have fallen into the comparison trap. You are competing against others when you need to be competing against yourself. The only person you need to be better than is the person you were yesterday."

Mary wasn't convinced. "But I want to sell 12 houses in my first year, and I'm still spinning my wheels. Yes, I'm getting more confident, but I don't have any clients to even show how confident I am!"

"I hear you," Neil said. "Have you ever seen the movie

Karate Kid?"

"Yes, of course."

"Remember how Daniel just wanted to fight, but Mr. Miyagi had him wax the cars, paint the fence, and sand the deck? Why? So, when it was time to fight, he had what he needed. Right now you are painting the fence, and you are annoyed by it. All you want to do is just fight and win. You want to learn karate, not paint the stupid fence."

Another light bulb went off for Mary.

Neil went on, "You operated for months without a clear plan. You floundered and tried many different things and didn't stay consistent with any of them. That is changing for you now. You are getting a clear plan, you are building your business, you are painting the fence. Even though you might not see it right now, it will pay off."

Neil paused, giving Mary time to ponder what he had said.

After a moment, she spoke. "You are so right. A few weeks ago I had no idea where I was going. I believed since I hated cold calling I would never be successful. I'm not successful yet, but I'm a lot further along now then I was back then."

"Exactly! Now we just keep working your plan. And we keep documenting your growth. Later in the Agent Rise Steps™, I will show you how to track your business so you are always competing against yourself and not others."

12. My friend listed with someone else!

Mary came to the next meeting with Neil absolutely heart broken. The night before she found out that a really good friend of hers from high school just listed her house with another agent.

Mary slumped in her chair and didn't even look up. "I feel like giving up," she said. "If my good friends won't list with me, who will? I'm not even sure this business is right for me."

"It hurts, doesn't it?" Neil said softly.

"Yeah. It hurts a lot."

"Did I ever tell you about the best man from my wedding?"

"No."

"I found out he listed with someone else. My best man! I could hardly function for weeks. If my best man wouldn't list with me, who would?"

Mary looked up. "So it happened to you too."

"Yep. And do you know what else? It's happened to almost every real estate agent. We've all gone through this. But here's the truth: Almost always, it has nothing to do with you—especially when you're new. Your friend probably already had a relationship with another agent before you decided to become one."

Mary nodded.

Neil went on. "In addition, some people prefer not to do business with friends. Strange to us, maybe, but reality for them. In the case of my best man, he was building a home and the agent who represented the builder said he would sell his home for free if he built with them."

"Wow! That's a hard offer to turn down."

"Yes, it is. But the bottom line is this: It had nothing to do with me. It had nothing to do with my abilities. And the same is probably true for you if, and when, one of your friends works with a different agent. People have their own reasons."

"That's reassuring," Mary said.

"And there's another aspect to this. There's a tough reality we all must face: We are not entitled to everyone's business. Just because we have a relationship with them, have been friends for so long, mail them our newsletter, are in a small group together at church, or whatever—does not mean we have earned their business."

"But I should still work on my Sphere of Influence, right?"

"Absolutely! Over time your sphere will yield a big portion of your business. Just because one or two friends go elsewhere does not mean you give up on your sphere."

"Okay."

"The bottom line here is this: Don't let anyone determine your identity based on whether they list with you or not. You are an amazing person and an amazing real estate agent. It was God's provision for your friend to list with someone else. God will provide for you. Just rest in that truth."

13. Chase Pillar™ & lead generation

Once Mary established her Sphere of Influence Pillar by building her database of 89 households, sent her announcement letter, and put her first newsletter in the mail; it was time to get busy on building her Chase Pillar™—Step 4 in the Agent Rise Steps™.

Neil went through the different options available in the Chase Pillar™—including open houses, online leads, Facebook Ads, FSBOs and Expireds, geo farming, or a niche. The two of them decided on open houses. They fit Mary's outgoing personality and her love of meeting people in person. In addition, open houses were more affordable for her at this time.

"Okay," Mary said. "Of all the choices, open houses seems like the best choice. But I'm not convinced it's a good choice. I've done them in the past—as you know—and the results have been less than stellar."

"Less than stellar?"

"I have never obtained a client through an open house. Not one. Not even close. I'm also not so sure I want to work every weekend. I will if I need to, but I don't want to do it if it's not going to bring money in."

"I get that. And I don't blame you. But let's figure out

why open houses didn't work in the past, and what you can do to fix it. Okay?"

"Okay."

"Here's how most people do open houses. They set out twenty open house signs and bake cookies the night before. They record a Facebook live to tell all their friends to come. Maybe they knock on the doors of the thirty closest neighbors. Then they set up everything inside the house. By the time the open house rolls around, they're already exhausted. But they can't be, because they need to have it all together when people walk through the door. But many times no one shows up, or, if people show up, everyone has an agent, so you don't get any leads. Rinse and repeat the next weekend. Sound familiar?"

Mary laughed out loud. "How did you know?"

Neil smiled. "I've been there. But here's what we're gonna do instead. We're gonna keep your open houses super simple so you can do one, two, or even three a week without breaking a sweat."

"How? How do you keep it simple and still get people to show up?"

"Most people come to an open house because they saw it online. The home needs to be on the MLS at least 48 hours prior to the open house so it shows up on all major search sites. Set up about three to five directional signs with a rider on the top with the hours you'll be open. Post a big flag in the yard that says, 'Open House.' Don't door knock. Door knocking works for some people, but not for you. It's not your personality, and you won't stay consistent with it. Plus, you don't want to exhaust yourself doing something you don't want to do anyway. And don't bake cookies. Instead, go to Costco and buy granola bars, protein bars, small packs of cookies, bottled water. Buy this in bulk. Set up a bunch when you arrive. Keep it simple."

"That is a lot easier."

Neil continued, "As far as Facebook lives go, it's great to let your followers on Facebook know that you are busy and are out there working, but no one is going to see your live and say, 'Honey, look Mary is doing an open house today, let's go see her!' Seriously, that won't happen. Now again it's great to have your followers see that you're busy, but it's time we do social media on purpose."

"Oh, my! What a relief!" Mary said. "I hate doing those Facebook lives, and you're right I have never had anyone come because they saw my live."

"It's not your strength. That's why it never felt right."

"Exactly!"

"Now, don't get me wrong. You still want to post on Facebook about the open house. Advertise the house and it's features. Lead with something compelling like 'Are you dreaming about a new kitchen? You have to see this one at our new listing at XYZ address!' Then show amazing photos of the kitchen. And include in the post the open house times."

Mary was jotting down notes as Neil continued.

"However, don't make the mistake of making the ad about you doing an open house. Then it's just about you, about how hard you're working. Instead, you want to show evidence of success. When people see your listing, something clicks in their minds: Others are trusting you. Now they can too. Make sense?"

Mary looked up from her notes. "Yeah. I've been doing it all wrong. I've been leading with: 'Come see me this weekend at my open house.' All about me. I'm working. I need to put the accent on the house. That will build trust."

"Right on!" Neil took a sip of coffee and then continued: "You'll want an open house flag outside whipping in the wind—one that says 'Open House.' Get some jazz music playing to give the environment a rich sound. Light a simple candle to give the air a fresh smell. Turn every light on. And place a small chalkboard sign outside that reads, 'Welcome! We are open until 3 pm today.' Add a smile to your face, and you're all set."

"Okay."

"Next we want to look at your process. What do you currently do when people walk in?"

"Maybe I don't have a process. I mean I don't really know what to do. I just greet them and show them around."

Neil nodded. "That's what most agents do. Most agents let leads slip through their fingers because they don't have a process. Instead, they wait for that moment when they become best friends with someone, get excited, and then go off looking for homes together. But let's be realistic. How often does that happen?"

"So far, it hasn't happened for me."

"Right. And guess what? It rarely happens for other agents as well. So let's go at this a different way. Most people who come to open houses are cold. It's hard to start a conversation. What do you say?"

"I'm not sure."

"Instead of letting one lead after another slip away because you are chasing that magical moment, we're going to look at every person who walks through that door as someone you can serve. Let me show you how you set that up."

"Okay!" Mary's pen was poised to take more notes.

"First, go buy twelve small, half-page clipboards. Use the Agent Rise "Open House Sign-in Sheet."[8] Have twelve clipboards ready to go. Put five or so in your arm. When people walk in the door, shake their hand, and hand them a clipboard. Ask them to complete the survey as they walk through the house.[9]

---

[8] Visit agentrisecoaching.com/resources for your copy of the "Open House Sign-in Sheet."

[9] This process was developed prior to the Covid pandemic. In a pandemic, you'll need to make adjustments to this process to make it Covid compliant.

"Another thing: Don't follow them through the house. Stay right where you are, so you are there for the next person who walks in the house, and you are there when they come back to give you the clipboard.

"When they do, then ask one question: 'What did you like most and what did you like least about the house?' This will draw the buyer's search criteria out from them. They will say something like, 'We love the back yard and the three-car garage, but we really need a 4th bedroom.'"

"I like this already," Mary said.

"So you see the magic here, right? Now we know the buyer wants a four-bedroom house with a nice back yard and a three-car garage. Then we can follow up with questions about desired location, price, size, and so on."

"I love it!"

"Most agents focus on how many people come to their open house and how many people they get contact information from so they can follow up on Monday. Instead we want to focus on how many criteria you acquired. Because once you have their contact information and search criteria, you can serve them. You can give them what they want ... a house!"

"Sweet!"

"And where will you get the contact information? On the clipboard! They're already filling it out for you.

"Again, most agents are waiting for that magical moment where you become best friends. You no longer need to do that. Now, just focus on getting search criteria and contact information. Once you have those two things, you can now give them what they want. You can now Match-Make with them."

"Wow! Now I know why I didn't like doing open houses. I was doing them all wrong. I was waiting for that magical moment that never came. I love this approach, Neil. This opens a whole world of possibilities I didn't even know was there."

14. Matchmaking & lead conversion

"Let's talk about Matchmaking," Neil said. "On Monday, most agents will call and follow up with everyone who attended the open house. They call and leave a message that sounds something like this, 'Hi this is Jane Doe from XYZ Realty Company, and I wanted to thank you for coming to our open house. I just wanted to check in and see if there is anything I can do or any questions I can answer. Give me a call back when you get a chance.'"

Mary laughed. "Oh, yes! I've left many messages like that. And they never call back."

"No, they don't. And here's why. The customer doesn't want to keep you in the loop. They don't need to update you. You're one of five agents they met this last weekend. Why would they ever call you back?"

"Yeah. Now that I think about it, I would never call back either!"

"So they don't return our call. We take that personally, and we don't ever call them again. We let one lead after another slip through our hands. This is why so many agents don't do well at open houses, and this is why we struggle to even want to do them.

"So we need to turn this around. When we make that

call on Monday morning, let's call that buyer with what the buyer wants—a HOUSE! Since we already have their contact information and their search criteria, let's find something that matches what they're looking for. Then we can call them and say something like this:

"'Hi, this is Mary from City Realty. We met over the weekend at the open house. You were telling me that you're looking for a four bedroom, two bath home with a three-car garage in Royal Oaks. I just saw one pop up, and I thought of you. Give me a call back when you get a chance, and I will tell you more about it.'"

"Wow! What a light bulb moment!" Mary said. *I can't believe it,* she was thinking. *No wonder no one ever called me back. I wasn't giving people what they wanted. This is going to make things so much easier.*

"Isn't it though! Instead of asking the buyer to serve you by updating you and contacting you, you are serving the buyer by giving them what they want. It's easy and fun to give people what they want."

"I can't wait to do my next open house!"

"This will make it so much easier. Now let's talk about how to keep track of the information you gathered at the open house. I recommend you add the information you gather to a spreadsheet. Here's how you organize that spreadsheet. Column A: location. Where—what neighborhoods or what communities—are they looking? Column B: price range. Column C: name and contact information. Column D: search criteria. Number of bedrooms, or whatever. Then sort your sheet alphabetically by Column A—location. This way, when you find a property in a certain location, you can quickly see what buyer this property might be a match for."

Neil showed her an example:

	A	B	C	D
1	Location	Price Range	Name and Contact Information	Search Criteria: Number of Bedrooms, Baths, Neighborhood, Attached Garage etc.
2				
3				
4				
5				

"Hmm," Mary said, "Does this mean I can get rid of CRM?"

"No, keep your CRM. Customer Resource Management software provides a number of automations and benefits like email property alerts that this spreadsheet can't provide. But the spreadsheet allows you to see all of your potential buyers at a glance."

15. Stacking lessons

Over the next two weekends, Mary did three open houses. She went into them super excited, and walked away defeated.

"From the three open houses," she said to Neil, "I only got one criteria. Just one. I feel like such a failure. I don't think I am cut out for this. I did three open houses and got one search criteria!"

Neil shook his head. "No. Failure isn't possible unless you quit. When you invest your effort toward a goal, you either get the result you are going for or you get a lesson. Then you take those lessons, and you stack them up until you reach the results you are looking for. With that in mind what lessons did you learn?"

"That I suck at open houses!"

They both laughed.

Then Neil said, "No, no, no; that's not true. Where did you do the open house—what price range?"

"One was a new construction for Johnson Builders."

"Let's stop there. Don't do open houses for new construction. They are open all the time and have no urgency behind them. Plus did it even get put on the MLS?"

"I'm not sure. I didn't know new construction was a bad idea."

"Okay, so we learned two lessons. Number one: Don't do open houses on new construction, and number two: Make sure the open house date and time are on the MLS at least 48 hours before the open house. Here's why: About 90% of your potential customers will find out about your open house from the MLS. What else did you learn?"

"The other one I did was an older listing that has had a few open houses already and slower traffic."

"There's a place for doing older listings," Neil said. "I generally don't mind doing open houses with these older listings as buyers who are just getting in the market are catching up to the inventory and looking at older listings to start—the same listings that the hot buyers passed on already. The hot buyers usually have agents already, and are hungry for the brand new listings."

Mary looked down and shook her head. "That's the biggest problem, Neil—everyone already has an agent. They had an agent before they walked in the door."

Neil nodded. "Did you ask every buyer if they had an agent?"

"Yes, of course, that's what I was taught to do."

"Well, here's another lesson: Whenever you ask a buyer if they have an agent at an open house, they will usually say yes. They know that if they say yes you will leave them alone. Instead, rely on the clipboard. One of the questions on the clipboard is: 'How did you discover this listing?' And one of the options to circle is 'my agent.' If they circle this, I then ask them, 'Who is your agent?' If they say Peggy from RE/MAX, I'll say great, you are in good hands with Peggy, she'll take great care of you. But..."

Neil paused for a moment, and then continued. "...but if they struggle to say their agent's name, usually it's a sign they don't have an agent. Obviously you don't want to call them out, instead you roll with it, but approach them a different way... I follow up by asking them if they have signed a buyer agency agreement with said agent."[10]

Mary was taking notes now.

Neil continued, "If they haven't signed anything, I will then ask the following question: 'We have houses that are not yet available on the MLS.[11] Would you like to know about them before they come to the market?' In a market

---

10 Important: Make sure you follow your state's laws and check with your broker on when and how you need to ask a buyer if they have an agent. Also, remember your main duty is to sell the house you are hosting the open house in. By asking visitors what they like most and least you will also pick up on their level of interest in the home.

11 Please note that "not yet available on the MLS" doesn't mean "coming soon" (although it can). What we really mean by "not yet available on the MLS" is houses that don't have listing contracts—FSBO's, expired listings, neighbors you met that are thinking about selling, a friend who wants to sell but hasn't signed a listing agreement, and so on.

with such low inventory, they can't resist, and will almost always say yes to that question. Then you reply with, 'Great, do you want me to call you with them or should I call your agent?' They most likely will say, 'Just call me.' If they do, you now have permission to call them.[12]

"This same strategy works if the buyer didn't put down her phone number. When you ask if she wants to know about houses not the MLS, and she says yes, then just say, 'Great! Can I get your phone number so I can call you with those houses?'"

Mary laughed. "It sounds to me like years of experience behind these words."

Neil smiled. "You know it. So to recap, we have stacked some lessons now, haven't we? You'll stack more along the way, but you are getting the hang of it!"

"That's encouraging."

"So, Mary, do you have any open houses set up for this weekend?"

"Not yet. I'm waiting to see what comes available. I've been doing open houses for a couple of the top listing agents in our office. I'm just waiting to hear from them to see if they have anything for me."

"Oh wait! Here's another lesson: When you call a top

---

12 Again, check with the laws in your state and talk with your broker to make sure you are following the correct procedure in your state.

listing agent and ask if they have an open house available, they are only thinking about their immediate need to cover one or two that they need. Most of the time they have teammates to cover them, and so, in their mind, they're all set.

"So instead of asking them if they have any available, go to the MLS and look up your company's inventory. Find the house you would like to do an open house on. The one in the price range you want and in the area that you want to focus on. Then reach out to that listing agent about that specific house. Send a text—something like: 'May I do an open house on your listing at 123 Main St?' The listing agent will specifically think about the status of that listing and will say, 'Sure, go right ahead, it's vacant.' See what just happened? The listing agent didn't have a need, but when you ask specifically about a property her mind goes directly to that listing. Now you make the listing agent look good to their seller. The listing agent can say to the seller: 'We want to spark more activity so we are going to do an open house this weekend.' It's a win win for everyone."

"Wow! There really is a science to this, isn't there?" Mary then added, "The other challenge I ran into last weekend was that one of the open houses I had scheduled got an accepted offer before the open house."

Neil said, "Oh yes, that is going to happen. The best way to prevent that from happening is to ask the listing agent to present offers after the open house, but that's not up to the listing agent—that's the sellers choice. If that is not an option, and often it's not, then the best thing to do is to do the open house in the evening during the week within 48 hours of listing. Enough time for the listing to circulate advertising the open, yet not too much time for it go under contract yet. List on a Tuesday and do an open house on Thursday evening from 4 to 6 pm."

Mary's coffee was getting cold by the time she finally took her first sip. But she barely noticed. "I need to say it again: Wow! I came in here ready to throw in the towel on open houses and switch to Facebook ads. But now I see there's a much smarter way to do this."

"I'm glad you're sticking with open houses. I think that's the best fit for you. If you switched to Facebook ads, then you'd need to start all over with stacking lessons. Remember: You don't fail at anything, unless you quit. When you quit, you wipe out all the lessons. But when you have lessons, then—when you try again—you can work smarter. When you give up and switch to a different strategy, you end up starting over. Most of the lessons you learned don't transfer. We call this 'switch cost,' and you want to avoid switch cost as much as possible."

16. Cracking the open house code

The weekend went fantastic. Mary hosted two open houses and couldn't wait to get on the phone with Neil Monday morning.

"I did it!" she told him. "I got seven criteria this weekend!"

You could feel the warm enthusiasm in Neil's voice. "That is awesome! Way to go! What lessons did you learn with it? What are your takeaways?"

Mary paused for a moment to think. "Let me see. These were priced right around the median price. One had been on the market for 11 days with no offers. Using your system, I was able to determine that many of these buyers didn't have agents. One of them actually wants to look at another house with me tomorrow night!"

"Awesome! Go go go!"

"Thank you so much. Let me just review with you what I should do with the other buyers."

"You'll enter their criteria in a spreadsheet and organize them based on location. Next, you'll want to start searching for houses that are not on the market or houses that just came to the market. Call your buyers with these houses and say, 'I saw this one, and I thought of you.'"

"Yeah," Mary said. "with the inventory so low it's hard to find houses for these people."

"In a low inventory market, you'll need to focus on finding houses that aren't yet on the MLS."

"How do you do that?"

"You can start with FSBOs on Craigslist and Facebook Marketplace. In addition, you can send out letters on your buyers' behalf to homeowners in appropriate neighborhoods. I also recommend sending letters to Expireds[13] from a few years back that didn't sell. And sometimes you meet a few neighbors at open houses who are thinking about selling, and give you permission to tell people about their home." Neil paused for a sip of coffee before continuing.

"In a low inventory market like this, many times the house won't be an exact match, and that is okay. Reaching out to them and giving them something close to what they want will compel them to work with you. After matchmaking like this for a while, you'll have buyers calling you to see if you can show them a house. You will no longer need to convince them to work with you, they will be asking to work with you."

"Don't I need their permission to look for houses?"

"Yes and no. Technically, you shouldn't call anyone that

---

13 Visit agentrisecoaching.com/resources for "Buyer Expired Letter Email Template."

doesn't want you to call them or someone who is on the do not call list. Of course, respect that. Beyond that, it's totally okay to call someone to give them something they are looking for (a house that matches their criteria). I believe agents overcomplicate this. You are simply listening to what they want and calling them to give it to them. Nothing more, nothing less. You're serving the public, that's it."

"I never looked at it that way. I guess I was over complicating it. I always would try to get an appointment with them and see if we could work together before I did anything else."

"You wanted to become best friends with them first."

"I did."

"Remember to just keep it simple. Get their contact information and their search criteria. Then call them with houses that match what they are looking for."

"Okay, good to know. Should I keep doing open houses? Or are these seven criteria enough for now?"

"Short answer? Yes, keep doing open houses. You need to know, at most, 20% of good-to-great leads will actually close. So with seven criteria, you're looking at one—maybe two—deals out of that."

"Aww, I was expecting all seven to be deals."

Neil laughed. "In a perfect world yes, but in reality no, not that many will close. But let's pretend they did. How does the thought of having seven transactions going at once feel to you?"

"Overwhelming."

"Overwhelming?"

"Yeah! It freaks me out."

"Why does that scare you?" Neil asked.

"I don't know. I'm just afraid I won't know how to manage all of that."

"I get that. It's new and unknown territory. But there can also be a fear of success here. And that will hold you back from stepping into the territory you need to conquer in order for you to succeed in this business. Fear of success is one fear that most people never think of, and truthfully it ruins more businesses than the fear of failure. Fear of success puts many of us in positions of limiting ourselves and depriving ourselves of the opportunities that yield the massive results we truly desire. We end up wanting success, but we're too afraid to go after it."

"Ouch!" Mary said. "That hits close to home."

"Many people wrestle with this. Do you want to know how to get over it?"

"Absolutely!"

"Good news! You've already completed the first step. You're aware of it. You acknowledge it. Most people don't even know about this or can't even admit they struggle with it. So you're already miles ahead of the herd."

"Okay."

"Next we need to understand something. To achieve a new level of success you need a new set of skills."

"For example?"

"Six months ago, you didn't know how to write an offer to purchase. You didn't need to know that then. But you need that knowledge now, and you have it. Information is provided as we need it. We learn as we grow."

"Okay."

"God is a God of abundance. He wants you to receive as much as you are ready to receive. Every step of the way He will provide for you. He knows how to remove that fear of success. How will He do that? You merely need to believe that what you need will be provided for you as you grow."

"How do I learn to believe that?"

"To form any belief, you must have evidence to support that belief. If you look for it, you'll find the evidence. And here's some evidence right now: You have survived everyone of your bad days. Think about it! You have a history of getting what you need when you need it."

"Wow! You're right!"

"You need to choose what evidence you're going to believe. You can believe the evidence that supports your belief that you will get the information you need when you need it. Or you can believe the evidence that supports the fear that you won't be able to handle success when it comes."

"Well, that just sounds silly to even say that. Of course, I'll learn and grow, and I'll get what I need when I need it."

"Fantastic! I see you doing very, very well. We just need to mix together the right recipe for your success. Belief is one ingredient. Knowledge is another ingredient. Next time we'll talk about another important and often undervalued key ingredient ... systems."

17. Systems

Over the next few weeks, Mary—buoyed by the belief she will acquire the information she needs when she needs it—moved forward with open houses and started connecting with more potential buyers. Pretty soon she was matchmaking for 24 buyers using the techniques Neil suggested.

Between matchmaking and working with her sphere of influence (one of her good friends became a buyer), Mary was finally beginning to break through. Things were coming together. Two deals were pending and she was about to write up an offer on a third.

But with success came a new problem. She was totally stressed out.

What if I let people down? she thought. *I'm spinning too many plates! How do you keep track of multiple deals at one time?*

When she brought this challenge to Neil, he said, "This is totally normal. You're in new territory. What got you here, will not get you where you're going. But don't worry; you'll learn what you need along the way. Don't let your current limitations sabotage your future growth. No, you don't know how to manage multiple deals because you've never done it. But you will learn what you need when you arrive."

"Okay... How?"

"You've reached a point where you need systems. Having systems in place will increase your confidence. Remember: Confidence is a muscle. It's not one of those things you either have or don't have. It's something we all have. Some just have more than others. You can change how much confidence you have by exercising confidence. You can strengthen that muscle."

"I highly recommend having a transaction coordinator after your first 10 deals. The only reason I recommend doing 10 deals without a transaction coordinator is so that you learn how to complete a transaction on your own. That way, if you need to do it on your own, you can. You won't be dead in the water if something happens to your transaction coordinator."

"I've heard you should only hire a transaction coordinator if you get really busy," Mary said.

"That's conventional wisdom," Neil replied. "But I disagree. I say this: You won't get busy until you hire a transaction coordinator."

Neil continued, "One time I was out boating, and the boat wouldn't plane out. I thought there was something wrong with my engine. When I turned back to look, I noticed that my back anchor was still down! It was dragging behind the boat. That is exactly what it's like running this business without a transaction coordinator. It's pulling you down."

"Okay. I can look into hiring a transaction coordinator after I close a few more deals. Meanwhile, I still need help. There's too many loose ends."

"No problem. In your Agent Rise™ resources, you'll find an email template[14] for you to send to your buyers after an accepted offer. In addition, for managing contingency deadlines, you can go as simple as a spreadsheet with deadlines on it, to using your CRM, to putting the deadlines in your calendar. Once you have a transaction coordinator, they will do all of this for you, but for now you need to do it yourself. Keep a checklist ready to go when you get a new buyer."

"Okay," Mary said, "What about sellers? I have a listing appointment next week, and I'm really nervous about it because the last one didn't go very well."

"No worries," Neil responded. "In fact, listing appointments often bore sellers because most agents are never trained to do them properly. Most agents are not trained to emotionally connect with their sellers during the listing appointment."

"I assume you're about to teach that to me."

"Of course! The first thing to understand is this: Turn your *listing* appointments into *listening* appointments. When sellers feel heard and understood, they'll want to work with you. Most agents go in and spend the entire time

---

14 Visit agentrisecoaching.com/resources for your copy of "Buyer Accepted Offer Email Template."

presenting to the seller to convince them of how great they are. The homeowner is bored out of their mind listening to this. After the agent leaves, the sellers are most likely losing sleep at night because they're worried about what to fix before they list, if they'll have enough money to buy their next home, how long it will take to sell, the weird neighbor next door that they don't want to come into their home, and all the other questions they had that the agent never heard and never answered. In short, they have concerns, and if we're too busy talking about how great we are, we will lose them. But you won't do that, will you?"

"No, sir!"

Neil smiled. "Of course not! I'll show you five different ways to get at your sellers' concerns. By asking compelling questions, you will learn how to best serve them, set expectations for a smooth transaction, and build one raving fan after another."

Neil placed a document on the table and continued. "Here are the steps you want to follow: Step one: Send an email. As soon as you hang up the phone from setting the appointment to meet at their home, focus on getting valuable intel on the seller before you meet face-to-face. Before your meeting, send the seller an email that includes a questionnaire. It's good to get some of the hard-to-ask questions out of the way before your appointment. For example, if you've ever asked a seller face-to-face what they want to price their home, you've probably been met with: 'Well, isn't it your job to determine the price?' or 'I want to hear what you think, first.' Your questionnaire avoids all that poker-hand awkwardness."[15]

Mary looked over the questions and nodded. "I like these," she said.

Neil continued, "In your email, you'll also want to include your marketing plan. Sending your marketing plan ahead of time means you don't have to bore them with it during your appointment. Keep it brief so you customize the plan as you learn more about what your seller does and doesn't like.

"And, of course, you'll want to confirm the date and time of your meeting."

Neil turned the page to the sample email. It looked like this.

> Hello [First Name(s)] -
>
> It was great to meet you over the phone today, and I truly look forward to helping you sell your home. [INSERT MORE PERSONAL INFORMATION BASED ON YOUR CONVERSATION]
>
> As promised, attached is a look at our marketing plan, all of which will be customized for your sale. If you get a chance, please look it over

---

15 It's easy to set up a questionnaire like this in Google Forms or Typeform.

prior to our meeting.

In addition, I've put together a quick questionnaire so I can get to know you better. When you have a moment, can you please answer the following questions?

[INSERT YOUR LINK TO QUESTIONNAIRE]

I look forward to meeting you at [TIME] at [LOCATION].

Have a great day!

[Your Name]

"Can I get a digital copy of this?" Mary asked.

"Absolutely! I'll also send you a copy of the questionnaire." Mary and Neil looked over that document as well. Here's what it looked like:

The Pre-Appointment Questionnaire

In addition to the basics like name and contact information, ask questions like:

• What attracted you to your home when you bought it? (This brings up happy memories for the seller, and helps you market what's important to them.)

• At what price do you think your home will list and sell for? (Again, this is the easiest, least uncomfortable way to draw out the seller's expectations.)

• What are your concerns or questions about the home selling process?

• We want our motivation to match YOUR motivation! On a scale of 1 to 5, with 1 being "just thinking about" to 5 being "get my house sold today," where would you rate yourself?[16]

"I wish I would have had this when I did my first listing appointment," Mary said.

"No worries," Neil replied. "You keep getting better and better at this—that's what matters. And, speaking of appointments, here's what you need to know. First of all, start your listing appointment at the kitchen table. Don't start with a tour of the house."

"Why not?"

"Because you want to establish trust and rapport before you start looking at the home. Here are a list of questions

---

[16] Agent Rise members receive a 25-question pre-appointment questionnaire and marketing plan template. Visit agentrisecoaching.com to learn more.

you want to ask." Neil slid another document across the table to Mary, and they read it together.

> Questions to ask at the listing appointment:
>
> Have you sold a house with a REALTOR® before? If so, how did it go? What did you like most about that experience? What frustrated you most?
>
> What's the one thing I need to do that will make our relationship and the process awesome—and give you the motivation to refer me to your family and friends?

At this point, Neil broke in. "You want to reinforce expectations and get more insight into what the seller is looking for in an agent. It's also nice to drop in that referrals are important to you."

They both smiled. And then they went on reading:

> What marketing on other listings have you seen that you appreciate?
>
> How do you feel about open houses?

"These last two are important," Neil said, "because you want to avoid talking to your seller about approaches they don't care about. And you do want to specifically ask about open houses. You want to learn if this marketing option is even on the table. I once spent a ton of time talking with a seller about how we do open houses with excellence, and they didn't want an open house. They almost listed with another agent."

Neil turned back to the document and said, "These last questions are important for setting expectations. You want to continue to establish trust and get additional insight from the seller."

> How long do you expect the sale to take?
>
> Do you have any questions?
>
> What about the sale worries you the most?

"It's so important," Neil said, "to connect with the seller on an emotional level. I suggest you slow down, get very serious with them, and ask 'What are you most worried about? What is keeping you up at night as you think through the process?' If you do this correctly, a wall will come down and there will be an emotional connection between you and the seller(s). Once you reach that emotional connection point with the seller(s), they are 99% going to be listing with you.

Most likely, they didn't reach that connection with any other agent.

"After this kitchen table Q&A, give a very brief overview of your marketing plan. Then you finish with this final question."

> Do I have your permission to be 100% honest with you when we're touring your home today?

"You need to get their permission, or risk insulting them. Only now do you move on to step three—a tour of their home."

"Okay, kitchen table before the tour. Got it!" Mary was taking notes.

"As you go through the seller's home, be generous with your expertise. Offer suggestions—and remember you have their permission to be honest! Some agents hold back on staging recommendations until the seller has signed a listing agreement. This is a mistake. By giving sellers advice before they've even committed to listing with you, they'll experience you as generous and helpful. Offer as much advice as they'll take."

"Okay."

"When the tour is over, you head back to the kitchen table for step four. Now it's time for you to win your listing!"

"How do you do that?"

"As you know, sellers often make the mistake of hiring whichever agent suggests the highest list price. You obviously don't want to inflate a price just to win a listing. (That never ends well). Fortunately, even if the seller's expectations are too high, you can still win their business—without overpricing."

"How?"

"You want to price the home *with* the seller. You don't want to present them with a price. You never want to say, 'I think your home will sell for X number of dollars.' If you do, you are setting yourself up to lose the listing. Instead, you want to go through MLS sheets and say something like this: 'This property sold for $320,000. After the adjustments,[17] that would make yours worth $323,000.' After you do this with every comparable property, then you say, 'After seeing all of this, what would you like to list your home for?'"

"So the seller sets the price."

"Exactly. That way it isn't your opinion vs. their opinion. Instead, you are educating them so they can make an informed decision."

"Okay."

"Once you've arrived at a price, then it's time to ask one

---

17 See the pricing adjustment resource at agentrisecoaching.com/resources.

more critical question: 'Now that we've determined the price, are you ready to work out our listing timeline and get the listing documents started?'"

"Make the sale…"

"Yes! Do not shy away from asking for the sale. You've added loads of value and you've listened well. You deserve this!"

"I love it!"

"It works so much better than the approach many agents take. Remember: When sellers feel heard and understood, they'll want to work with you! You don't want to waste this opportunity. The key here is to stop talking and start listening. When you do, you'll win more listings."

Neil continued, "Let me share a story with you about an agent I coached through this process. It happened like this. My agent received a call from the sellers that they were thinking about selling their house and belongings to go full time RVing. The agent sent the buyers a pre-listing questionnaire. The answers included when they wanted to move by, what they thought their house was worth, the concerns they had about juggling all of this, among other concerns they had with the process."

"So your agent had a lot of information going into the meeting."

"That's right. And all of this insight helped the agent position herself to best answer their questions and concerns.

They had previously interviewed two other agents. Both of these agents knew very little about what was on the sellers' minds—what was keeping them up at night. These agents came in and just talked about how great they were. They spent all of their time convincing the seller to list with them instead of answering their questions and concerns.

"The pre-appointment questionnaire set the tone for the meeting better than anything could. The pre-appointment questionnaire took the focus off how great the agent was and put it where it belonged—how much my agent cared about these sellers and their concerns. My agent won the listing by listening, by taking her sellers and their concerns seriously."

"Wow! That's fantastic!"

In addition to this listing system, Mary learned other systems during her meetings with Neil. These systems included a buyer consultation process, an email template for writing an offer with buyers, a different email template for presenting offers to sellers, and a contract-to-close process she could use immediately and, later, when the time came to hire her transaction coordinator.

At the end of their meeting, Neil handed Mary the *Agent Rise 12 Week Planner*. He explained that the planner would help her work according to a 12 Week Year[18] where we set 3 goals to accomplish in 12 weeks. Neil's system would allow Mary to track results using an engagement tracker (how

---

18 Suggestion: Read *The 12 Week Year* by Brian Moran.

many people called, met with, and sent thank you cards), along with a lead tracker (tracking the leads that come in).

"The planner will help you accomplish your three goals, while tracking your results, so then the only person you have to be better than is the person you were yesterday."[19]

---

19 Later in the Agent Rise Steps™, I will show you how to track your business so you are always competing against yourself and not others.

18. Believing the plan and forming habits

In the months that followed, Mary learned and implemented all of these systems. At first, it took a lot of work, but with Neil's help, she dialed them in. When she found a potential seller, her systems gave her a direct process that's clear and helpful to the seller.

And getting all these systems dialed in proved to be a game changer for Mary. While she has only had a limited number of listing (LISTENING) appointments, she was amazed at how much this process resonated with people. For example, neighbors from one of her open houses had a home to sell. They were interviewing two other agents and met Mary at the open house the week before they had appointments scheduled to interview the other two agents. Mary's timing was perfect. They loved how she presented the neighbor's house at the open house, and how the vibe and organization of her open house was on point. They practically started interviewing Mary that Saturday afternoon. She went to the appointment the following week. She was the last one they were interviewing. Mary sent the questionnaire ahead of time, and then followed it up with asking more questions at the kitchen table. Their comments? "You're the only agent who asked us questions. You're the only agent who listened to us, and the only one who seemed to care. I can see you are really eager to earn our business, and I didn't see any of that with the other agents we interviewed. In fact, meetings with them were all about them and how great they were."

During that appointment, Mary also noticed how the walls came down when she asked them, "What are your worries with this process?" They were able to share their fear that the house wouldn't sell for what they needed. In addition, the mortgage process was so much more complex than when they bought 10 years ago—leaving them to wonder if they would even qualify for a new mortgage. They didn't mention this to the other agents because the other agents never asked. They just talked about themselves.

Once Mary got this feedback, she knew more than ever she was on the right track.

But something was troubling Mary. During her next meeting with Neil, she brought it up:

"I love meeting new people at open houses. But I really thought I would have better results by now. I thought I would have more people in homes. So I need to ask: Am I looking in the wrong place? Is there a better source of leads?"

"Wait a second," Neil said, "Why are you asking about other chases?"

"Well, the buyers I'm working with from open houses are not as ready as I would like them to be. Some of them aren't looking to buy for six months or even longer. But people tell me that the leads you get online actually want into a house right now."

"The way I look at it is this: The same buyers who are inquiring online are the same buyers who are attending open houses. But this brings up something far more important."

"What's that?"

"You don't believe in your plan, do you?"

Mary looked down. "Well... yeah... I do. But I was just wondering if there's something better."

"But that's just it," Neil said. "You need to stop looking for something better. Looking for something better is a distraction—a distraction that prevents you from focusing. You can't allow that to happen. Take the energy you are spending searching for something else, and put that energy towards matchmaking with the leads you do have."

"You're right," Mary said, "I'm doing a horrible job with matchmaking. I feel so lazy during the week. I work hard on the weekends doing open houses, and I follow up with the new leads as they come in, but then I kind of get lazy with matchmaking with them afterward."

"It sounds to me like you are sleeping in the harvest."

"What do you mean?"

"Let's say you're a farmer. You plow the field to get ready for planting. You plant the seeds. You nurture the seeds. The seeds grow into plants and produce a crop. Then you go to sleep—you then let all of the crop die in the fields. You would never see a farmer go on vacation during harvest season would you? No, you see that farmer busting their butts to get the crop in. That is what you are not doing. Instead you are sleeping in the harvest."

"Ouch! That hurts... But I think you're right. I need to work harder, don't I?"

"You only have so much energy. You don't want to waste it. That's why you need to stay focused. And you can stay focused by believing in your plan. Stop looking for other options. Remember, last time we met I shared with you that you have to have evidence that supports your belief. Well, in order to believe in your plan, you need to have evidence that your plan will work, right?"

"Yes, I think that's it: I need more evidence that this will work."

"I understand," Neil said. "You can't believe something without evidence that supports your beliefs, right?"

"Right."

"And do you have evidence to support your belief in your plan?"

"I do," Mary said, "but..."

"But?"

"But I've just been believing the wrong evidence."

"Exactly! You can either believe the evidence that supports that your plan will work, or you can believe the evidence that supports your plan won't work. Or, even worse, you can believe the evidence that another plan is better."

"Okay. That makes a lot of sense." Mary was taking notes.

Neil continued, "Once you believe in your plan, then it's all about forming habits to support that plan. Right now you have a conversion problem. You are doing a great job generating leads from open houses, now we need to form a habit around matchmaking."

"I couldn't agree more. I really struggle with staying consistent with matchmaking."

"Okay," Neil said, "then this is what we are going to do: I want you to do the following each day. First, search for properties for 30 minutes a day. Second, call 5 buyers a day to present houses to them. Third, send 3 letters to old expireds or neighbors on your buyer's behalf. Do you think you can do that?"

Mary paused to think about the commitment she was making. Then she replied. "Yes, I can do that!"

19. Attraction Pillar™

The next time they met, Neil said, "I have a question for you. Remember back when you first came to see me? Remember all that time you were spending on Instagram?"

"Yeah, how could I forget? I thought I would be Instagram famous. But it got me nowhere."

"Remember what I said to you at the time?"

"Yeah, you said, 'Don't wax the car when the transmission is broken. Don't focus on making your car look great when it doesn't run. The same goes for your business.'"

"Right. Well, we've fixed the transmission. The car runs. You're getting clients. You're closing deals. Now it's time to move on to building your third and final pillar—your Attraction Pillar™."

"So is it time to go back to Instagram?"

"Maybe. Maybe not. You have several options for your Attraction Pillar™, and we'll need to figure out the one that works best for you."

"Okay."

"The Attraction Pillar™ will look different for different people. You can focus on a social platform like Instagram.

You can focus on a searchable platform like YouTube. Or you can focus on a niche like first-time buyers."

"So...three choices?"

"Right. Let's look at a social platform like Instagram. What does it look like if you focus on Instagram? To begin with, you will want to follow the best at Instagram and those who can help you understand the platform. You will want to geek out with the best of them. Chelsea Pietz is my favorite for agents to follow. I also think Jerry Potter is another you can learn a lot from. Agents that you need to follow include Paul Wolfert, Pinky Benson, Mindi Kessenich, and Zach and Ally Fiegel."

Mary was scribbling notes as Neil continued.

"Next you want to do some hashtag research and determine what local hashtags do you need to be following. Next you want to follow Gary Vee's $1.80 rule—where you go into 10 hashtags, look at the top 9 posts, and leave your two cents (like and comment). 9 posts x 2cents x 10 hashtags = $1.80."

Mary smiled.

"You'll use the hashtag research to find and connect with people in your city—for local sales, and with other agents across the country—for a referral network and to empower you along the way."

"Okay."

"Next you'll want to come up with your content plan. I

think that plan should be to post 3-5 times a week, have an Instagram story running daily, post a reel 3-5 times a week, and IGTV video once a week."

"Another option for platforms could be Facebook. I think we all need to be on Facebook, but if you make Facebook your Attraction Pillar™, then you need to do much more than what most do on Facebook. For example, you might do a weekly Facebook Live show or you might do a weekly contest like I did. I called it Mathweg Monday Trivia or MMT for short. Here's how it worked: Every Monday I posted a video. On the video, I said, 'Happy Monday everyone! It's that time once again to play Mathweg Monday Trivia. Here is this week's question.' Then I posed a question. For example: 'Name something you might see at a Milwaukee Brewers baseball game.' Then I announced the prize: 'The first one to guess correctly wins a $25 gift certificate to...' and here I would name a local restaurant. Wanna guess how many views we got every week?"

"How many?

"Twenty-five hundred to 5,000 organic views every week, because person after person would comment. We would allow one guess per person per day. If no one guessed by the end of the day, we would give a clue on Tuesday morning, and again each day until we got the correct answer. The correct answer was determined by myself and two other teammates in my office. They were also the judges if a guess was close, and would help me come up with the clues on each day they were needed. They were called the MMT Police."

"What fun!"

"MMT created such a buzz in our community. No other agents were finding success in their business pages, but this page broke through the noise. I was able to meet over thirty people through game that later interviewed me to be their agent. It was wildly successful."

"That's incredible!"

"And why did it work? It worked NOT because I talked about how great of an agent I am. Instead I was just human. I was fun. This resulted in a relationship with the audience. Multiple times I had people contact me and say, 'I've been playing Mathweg Monday Trivia for a year, and am thinking about buying a house. You're a REALTOR®, right?'"

"That's amazing!"

"For the right person, a social platform can work quite well. But you can also get great results with a searchable platform. My favorite right now is YouTube. But for so long we did it wrong..."

"You did it wrong? How?"

"Like most agents, I felt the need to produce video. Any type of video will do. Create content to get attention. We all believed it was an attention game. The more attention, the more deals you get."

"So that doesn't work?"

"No, it doesn't."

"Why?"

"Because most agents post the wrong videos. Let me show you a list." Neil slid a document across the table to Mary, and continued, "These are the five types of videos agents are told they should produce."

Mary glanced over the list:

- Property videos
- Community videos
- Interview business owners
- Market reports
- Tips for consumers

"Here is the thing," Neil said, "these videos don't work anymore. They are just adding to the noise."

"Why is that?"

"Let's take them one at a time. Property videos are good for displaying a listing, and should be used for that purpose. But as an Attraction Pillar™, no. They might get you a lead here and there, but for the most part they don't perform long term."

"Okay."

"Community videos. I invested hundreds of hours in a video series called *I Love Madison Food Tournament*. We would select a food category, like cheeseburgers. Then we'd ask 'Who has Madison's best cheeseburger?' Everyone cast their votes—hundreds of favorites came pouring in. Then we narrowed that list down to the top ten. We took that list and turned it into a poll. Hundreds—maybe even thousands—of votes came pouring in. We then narrowed it down to the final four, and then the final two. Finally, we loaded a bus full of judges and went to eat burgers at those two restaurants. We created a video to document the entire day. The video views were amazing, we saw 10,000 plus on Facebook and another 3,000 plus on YouTube. The attention we got was so awesome. I became a local celebrity. I couldn't walk into a restaurant without being recognized. The video still ranks highest when you search 'Who has Madison's best cheeseburger?'"

Mary was open mouthed. "Wow!" she said. "That's amazing."

"But here's the thing," Neil replied, "I don't sell cheeseburgers. Think about it…someone searching 'who has Madison's best cheeseburger' is looking for a cheeseburger, NOT a real estate agent. The same goes for videos about your favorite coffee shops, restaurants, diners, you name it."

"Oops…"

"Oops is right. Some agents are producing videos where they interview business owners. That doesn't work either.[20] Here's why: People don't care. Nobody really cares about the inside of someone's business, how it got started, what

---

20 Unless, possibly, you're selling commercial real estate.

they do, and so on. Most of the time it turns into an ad. And even if the story is interesting and entertaining to watch, the person who watches the video most likely isn't the same person searching for real estate or a real estate agent."

"Oh."

"Finally, take market reports. Of all things on the list, this is one that is closer to hitting the mark, only because the person who is searching for market information is probably interested in making a move. But here's the problem: Most people buy with their emotions. Consciously or unconsciously, they are asking themselves, *How is this move going to make me feel? What is my life going to be like once I move there?* They are NOT asking, *What is the current absorption rate? How many listings this month vs. last year?* People don't care. We care. Our clients don't."

"I guess that makes sense. What about advice videos?"

"I've tried those as well. 'Tips for consumers.' For example, a video on home inspections. Here's the problem with that. If they're searching for a video on home inspections, they don't need a real estate agent. They already have one. They're in the middle of a transaction."

"What about testimonial videos?

"It really depends on how they're done. Most of the time, they come off as commercials, and they turn people off. Once in a while, if you do it right, you can tell a story where you are the guide and not the hero—those can work. But they're not easy to do."

"So what do we post instead?"

"You need to start with the question: What are our ideal customers searching for? You need to think that through. For example, take this scenario: A potential client received an offer to move to Madison, Wisconsin. It's going to be a pay increase of $50,000 a year. But right now he lives in Indiana, and his cost of living is really low. He's wondering: *Is it worth it? Yes, I'll get a raise, but will all that increase just be gobbled up by a higher cost of living?*"

"You need to get inside the mind of your prospective client."

"Exactly! So what would he search? Would he search 'Who has Madison's best cheeseburger?'"

Mary laughed. "No!"

"Would he search 'Madison real estate market update'?"

"Probably not."

"No, he wouldn't. But he probably would search, 'cost of living in Madison, WI.'"

"That makes a lot of sense."

"Okay, another scenario. Who's the biggest corporate employer in the Madison area?"

"Epic."

"Right. Epic. So we have another person who has a job offer at Epic. They're coming from Minneapolis, and they need to figure out where to live. They're thinking—rent first, and then buy. They want to live in a hip, trendy area, and money isn't a major concern. If you were that person, what would you search?"

Mary thought about it for a moment, and then answered: "'Best places to live if you work at Epic'?"

"Bingo! You wouldn't be searching for interviews with a nonprofit CEO."

"This is starting to make sense."

Neil continued, "Here's another example. A prospective client needs to care for her elderly mom who really shouldn't be living on her own. She's trying to identify her options—in-home care, assisted living, whatever—but doesn't even know where to begin. What would this client be searching for?"

"I don't know. Maybe 'best places in Madison for aging mom.'?"

"Exactly. The key to YouTube is to identify your target audience, and ask yourself, *What questions does my target audience need answers to?* Find answers to those questions, and post those videos—not *What content do I want to produce that maybe my target audience would want?*"[21]

"Okay."

---

21 Want a list of most popular videos an agent can produce? Agent Rise members have access to this and many more templates inside Agent Rise Coaching. Go to agentrisecoaching.com to learn more.

"Another option with your Attraction Pillar™ is to work directly with a niche, and to put all your social media into what we call a social media ecosystem."

"What does that mean?"

"Let's use first-time buyers as an example. How do we attract first-time buyers? We've found the best lead magnet for this group is 'first-time buyer grants and down payment assistance (DPA) programs.' We offer a free post inside Facebook Marketplace that explains how grants and down payment assistance programs are now available. They click 'interested' and send a message in messenger. We then invite them to complete a questionnaire. From their answers we can guide them to a lender to see if they qualify for the grants or DPA. If they qualify we begin working with them. If they don't, we invite them to join our first-time buyer Facebook group. Then each month we conduct first-time buyer webinars. It's all about bringing them into the ecosystem, educating them, and encouraging them all the way up till the time they are ready to buy a house."

"Are there other niches?"

"Sure. Let's say that first-time buyers don't interest you and you'd rather work with another niche. We have ecosystems established for other niches including senior living, military, vacation rentals, divorce, probate, and investors."

Neil went on to explain other Attraction Pillar™ options. After some back and forth, Mary decided that YouTube made the most sense to her. She was excited to get started building her YouTube channel.

20. Sphere of Influence 2.0

A few weeks went by, and what a difference Mary's new habits made! She was so focused on matchmaking that she started getting swamped with deals. Three accepted offers in two weeks, plus a fourth she needed to write up later in the day. On top of that, she had a new listing coming up later in the week.

It was like Mary just flipped a switch and started putting deals together. She stopped looking at other options, and instead focused her attention on matchmaking. She put the Agent Rise Planner to use and so dialed in. She even surprised herself. Almost every day she spent at least 30 minutes searching for properties; some days it was even longer. Then she called at least five buyers to let them know she found a house and "thought of them." As a result she had no problem setting up one appointment a day—a showing, a buyer consultation, or a listing (LISTENING) appointment.

Now that Mary had her systems dialed in, formed habits, and believed in her plan, Neil decided it was time to take her Sphere of Influence Pillar™ to the next level.

Mary was doing a great job with her sphere already. For seven months she had mailed her newsletter consistently. She received great feedback and got calls and referrals on a normal basis from her sphere. Neil said she would get about 10% from her sphere. So if she had 100 people in a database she would get about 10 deals a year.

"Let's take that number up to 20%," Neil said. "Let me show you how to get twenty deals a year from the 100 people you have in your Sphere of Influence."

"How?"

"You're going to offer a VIP rental program to your clients. My second year as an agent I invested in an enclosed moving trailer. It was the best investment I ever made in my business. I had it wrapped with my name, logo, and phone number. And I put the words 'courtesy moving trailer ... use it for free!'[22] in big letters across the top of the side, front, and back of the trailer. I let anyone use the trailer. Besides being used by clients, it was also used by churches for youth group camping trips, high school football teams for camp storage, and even had the elementary school use it for a coat drive in the fall to store coats in. It went everywhere and was used all of the time. All with my name and number plastered all over it. Every time someone came to pick it up, my assistant or I met with them and had a great conversation about life and it always lead to us talking real estate."

After talking for a few minutes, they came up with a list of items Mary would offer:

---

22 Disclosure: consult with an attorney, insurance agent, and your broker in regards to a waiver of liability and the risk of renting items to people.

- a pressure washer
- an extension ladder
- a post hole digger
- a wheelbarrow
- some banquet tables and chairs that she bought from her church

At closing, she offered her clients a certificate saying they are now enrolled in her VIP program and would have access to those items for free.

She also invited her clients into a private VIP Facebook group. In the group, she announced new items she was adding to the "rental" program, along with random giveaways like "coffee on Mary." She also posted about events when she had them.

Soon Mary had added three components to her Sphere of Influence Pillar™ in addition to her monthly newsletter. So all together her sphere included:

- Monthly newsletters
- VIP rental program
- VIP Facebook Group
- Client events.

Mary and Neil talked for some time about scheduling client events. Neil explained, "Client events put you in touch with your clients even if they don't attend the event.

We send the invite (usually enclosed in our newsletter—with a stamp on the outside of the envelope that reads 'client event invite enclosed.' We advertise the event in two newsletters. Then following the event we included photos and an article about the fun at the event. Also, prior to the event we call all our clients to make sure they received the invite and to ask if they want to be added to the RSVP list."

Mary was scribbling notes.

Neil paused and added, "So even if they don't attend, we still get all of these amazing touch points with our clients. And if they do attend, you get to see them. You get to have fun with them. They see the human side of you and not just the busy real estate agent. They see you as a friend. They see how many other people have trusted you, and it reassures them you are the real deal. It helps them realize they need to be sending referrals your way."

As a result of that conversation, Mary planned her first event—Party in the Park—for late summer. Neil had done these events for years, and showed her exactly how to do it.

"Two fears," Mary said.

"Okay."

"The first is: How can I afford it? I can see this getting expensive real quickly. And second, what if I spend all this money and nobody shows up?"

"Understandable. Most agents feel the same way the first time they do events like this. Fortunately, there's an easy solution: co-op. Invite a couple of other agents in your office to participate in the event with you. All three of you invite people, and you share the cost. That way you'll have plenty of people there, and you won't need to worry about the expenses getting out of hand. None of your invited guests will need to know that not everyone in attendance was invited by you—that some guests are clients of other agents."

After a few minutes of planning, Mary decided that her Party in the Park would feature a catering company that would provide pulled pork sandwiches and fresh cut French fries. On top of that, she planned to offer a bouncy castle, face painting and other games for the kids. She would bring beer, soda, and other refreshments. And they would top it off with door prizes and other giveaways like t-shirts.

Mary set a goal of doing one event the first year—the Party in the Park. She would add additional events later, with a goal of two events her second year, three her third, and then four by year four. She and Neil brainstormed and quickly came up with a list of possible events. The list included:

- Baseball game at a minor league game in town
- Pumpkin patch event
- Bowling event
- Movie event at the local movie theater
- Drive up movie night

- Wine tasting event.

21. Clarity, congruency, and consistency

Mary was a little discouraged about her first client event.

"Only fourteen people showed up—six of whom were family," she told Neil. "I thought it would be much higher—after all, I invited 100 households—that's nearly 200 people plus kids. The other agents did a lot better than me—they each brought in about twenty five people. I was hoping I would do a lot better."

"Hey, you did fine," Neil said. "It's not about the people who didn't come. It's about the people who did come. You had fourteen. That's important."

"Okay."

"On top of that, you had a great point of contact with everyone in your database leading up to the event. You had the paper invite in their mailbox. You had two months of announcements for the event in your newsletter. You called everyone in your database with a good reason to call. You had multiple invites in your Facebook group. You have pictures from the event to add to your group. You had a great face-to-face time with the fourteen people who did come. All of this matters."

Mary smiled. "Well, since you put it like that, then I guess it was a success."

"Absolutely!"

Altogether, it took several months for Mary to understand and implement the Agent Rise Steps™, but once she did, things really began to fall into place. She had all the clients she wanted, and she was getting her buyers and sellers to the closing table regularly.

In the end, she had a clear plan that felt right for her. A huge moment in her breakthrough came when she got to the place where she believed in her plan. It helped to have Neil reinforcing her customized plan and being a part of the Agent Rise community. She was encouraged, and motivated, by watching the other agents working their own customized plans within the Agent Rise framework. That gave her the evidence she needed that she was on the right path.

In addition to her Three Pillar Plan™, she spends thirty minutes a day looking for properties to MatchMake with. Because she consistently has at least five conversations a day, and sets one appointment every day, her goal of getting one accepted offer each week is becoming a reality. Using the Agent Rise Planner has also helped her focus and work according to her vision.

She is completely dialed in. And for the most part her confidence is at 99%. She doesn't people please, she takes Sunday's off, her clients respect her, and she is having the time of her life.[23] Don't get me wrong there are still plenty of challenges, but if you asked Mary, she has built a business she loves.

And you can too!

* * *

Mary, of course, is a fictional character. But her story mirrors the experiences of Neil Mathweg's many Agent Rise Coaching™ clients. In Part Two of this book, we'll look at what the Agent Rise approach can do for your real estate career.

And before you read on, make one promise to yourself: Schedule a coaching discovery call at agentrisecoaching.com. It's free. It's 30 minutes. And it will change your business and change your life. I guarantee it, or your money back! 😊

---

23 In Chapter 31, "Set boundaries," I'll teach you how to set these boundaries so that you too can take Sundays off and have clients respect you. It's a real game changer.

Part Two: Your story

22. Your plan

Mary's plan is NOT necessarily your plan. Her plan works for her, your plan will work for you. Your strengths and weaknesses will be different than Mary's. For example, you might be new to the area and have a very small local sphere of influence. Or you may be more introverted, and the thought of doing one open house after another makes you sick. Can you still succeed?

Absolutely! But you need a plan that's congruent with your strengths, not Mary's. You need a plan that works for you. You can't spend your time doing things you hate. If you do, you won't be consistent. Once you have your plan, you must stay consistent with it.

The right plan + consistency = success.

Your breakthrough

Now is the time for you to go for your breakthrough. What is a breakthrough? It's going to a place you once found impossible to reach. With that in mind, breakthrough looks different for each person. It might mean beating the odds and "making it" in this business. With 87% of agents leaving the business in 5 years, breakthrough could mean being among the 13% who survive. Or maybe you're at a place in your business where you feel you have made it, but know that your potential is so much greater, and you feel stuck in trying to get there. Or maybe you've gotten your business to a level you desired, but now you wish you could breakthrough to get your life back.

Whatever situation resonates with you, aim for your breakthrough. And here's a little known secret: Most of the time you will experience a breakdown before you experience your breakthrough. It's just the way things tend to work.

As you can see with Mary, limiting beliefs can stand in the way of your breakthrough. Lies get into our heads blocking our achievements. Sometimes we convince ourselves we aren't qualified or good enough. When this happens we often pivot and go a different direction, avoiding our breakthrough moment and reverting to our old ways. When your breakdown comes—and believe me it will—you often need someone to pull you through to the other side—a coach who can see your blind spots, call out the lies, and convince you to keep going.

What breakthrough are you going for?

23. Simplify and Amplify

After 19 years of selling real estate and coaching hundreds of agents, one thing has come into focus as essential to your success:

Simplify and amplify.

You need a clear understanding of what you need to do every day to drive your business.

When most agents don't know where their next deal will come from, you will because you will have a clear plan.

Simplify. Do less. Absolutely.

But once you've simplified, amplify. Amplify what you've simplified. Do more of what works and less of what doesn't.

You might think: *Really? Do less? Why would I do that? You never know where the next deal is going to come from!*

I know the feeling. It's common to think that. And it's also common to fail in this business. Why do agents fail? #1 reason: They fail to simplify and amplify.

If I gave you enough lumber to build a bridge from one side of the river to the other side; would you use the lumber to build two half bridges that didn't connect? Or would you use the lumber to build a full bridge? You would use it to build one bridge so you can get to the other side, right? Of course! The lumber represents our time, energy, and focus in this business. Build one bridge. Simplify and Amplify.

Building your business is the same.

Build one bridge.

24. Agent Rise Steps™

Far too often I see agents spinning their wheels because they are doing things out of order. For example, they spend hours working on their appearance as an agent because they are following the other agents in the office that appear to have it all together. They look at the top agent in the office who has a logo, fancy business cards, custom built website (separate from the one given to you by your company), a Facebook business page, swag, and maybe even their car is wrapped. You see this, and you think—that's it. I need to get all of that done, because that will lead to my success.

Does that attract business? Of course it does. Branding and marketing are very important in this business, but if you're launching and building your business, this is the wrong place to start.

Let me share a secret with you. That awesome logo, the website, those custom designed business cards—they all have nothing to do with their success. They created all of that over time, with the money they used from things that are really driving their business.

It's like waxing your car when the transmission is broken. Fix your transmission so the car drives, then you can make it look pretty down the road.

Look at your business the same way. To get your business driving, follow the Agent Rise Steps™. Here they are:

25. Three Pillar Plan™

Like the Agent Rise Steps™, we came up with the Three Pillar Plan™ to help you develop a clear plan that is based on your unique combination of powers.

Too many coaching programs make agents fit into a box. I understand that every coaching program needs to have some structure, but too much structure suffocates the creativity and desire to be an entrepreneur.

I envisioned some structure because every good program must have some structure, but instead of the box being square, I envisioned a round box—one that gave you room for your powers, your gifts, your desires.

In each pillar, we give you a menu of options. That way you decide what is a best fit for you. Let's look at some of those options...[24]

Pillar #1: Sphere of Influence Pillar™

Your sphere of influence consists of your family, your growing circle of friends, former co-workers, and others who know you. If you take great care of your clients, this

---

[24] Get your copy of the Agent Rise Three Pillar Plan™ at agentrisecoaching.com/resources.

pillar ends up being 80% of your business as your career grows.

You want to keep your sphere updated, and bring them along with you on your journey.

We believe in the power of mailbox when it comes to reaching your sphere. I hear it all the time: "Shouldn't we just email our sphere? It's cheaper!" Yes, it's cheaper, but you get what you pay for. The email inbox is a noisy place where the desire to delete is much stronger than the desire to read. At best, you get a 30% open rate. At best. But the mailbox is not noisy. You might not get a 100% open rate, but you'll get far better than 30%. Everyone enjoys getting mail. And, unlike email, mail has a shelf life; it can continue to work for you days and sometimes weeks after you send it.

Am I saying you shouldn't do email marketing? Not at all. You can add email marketing later if you wish, but start with reaching your people through snail mail.

Most agents add email marketing in Agent Rise Step 8 when your Sphere of Influence Pillar™ will be amplified as you reach Sphere of Influence 2.0. But in the beginning, it's about reaching your sphere on a monthly basis. We'll add client events, emailing, videos, and much more as you build your business.

The first option in the sphere of influence pillar is to mail your own newsletter every month. The second option in the sphere of influence pillar is to mail a done-for-you newsletter like Service For Life. The third option in the sphere of influence pillar is to mail a letter from your heart each month. The fourth option in the sphere of influence pillar is to mail The World's Greatest Postcard. We help you build this in Agent Rise.

Pillar #2: Chase Pillar™

Your Chase Pillar™ is your engine. This is going to drive your business. Your Sphere of Influence Pillar™ and your Attraction Pillar™ are important, but it may take time before you see results from either of them. For the most part, they are the long game pillars, whereas your Chase Pillar™ is meant to get you quick wins.

If you're new, this will get your business going. If you are stuck, this is where we see most agents get unstuck.

It's a simple concept, but the work isn't easy. Agents typically need the most help with their Chase Pillar™. You may find this is where you need the most coaching and the most encouragement. It's the pillar that is the hardest to be consistent with. It's the hardest to reach mastery with.

Chase Pillar™ options: The first and most popular option is open houses. The second option is Facebook advertising. The third option is online leads. The fourth option is FSBO and Expireds hunting. And the fifth, and least popular, option is GEO farming.

Pillar #3: Attraction Pillar™

In your Chase Pillar™ you go after clients. In your Attraction Pillar™, you pull clients toward you.

Neat, right?

It can be. But first—fair warning: If you don't watch it, your Attraction can become a distraction.

I have seen agent after agent spend countless hours producing videos and podcasts and not receive a single piece of business from it. Your Attraction Pillar™ works, otherwise I wouldn't suggest it, but it takes time and you need to know the right and wrong way to do it. And if you put all of your energy toward it too early, your ship will sink.

I produced a show called *I Love Madison*. We documented Madison's restaurants, events, music, we hosted meetups and much more. We did video blogs—vlogs, we did food Tournaments, we hosted meetups with hundreds of people, we did everything you can think of. We did it with excellence. The first year we didn't work with anyone of the hundreds of people we met. The second year we sold one house from someone I met at a meetup.

Over time, this can turn into 3-5 houses, 5-10 houses a year, and more. But it takes time. If you put all your energy to this, you will starve.

You might have also noticed that the Attraction Pillar™ falls all the way down to number seven on the Agent Rise Steps™. Why? So it doesn't become a distraction.

I get why you might want to work on your Attraction Pillar™. It's fun! It's the recess of school. I love producing content and wish I could do it every day, all day.

But don't. Please don't. It will distract you from getting the results you need.

Your Attraction Pillar™ allows you to be an artist. You get to be creative. We all have art inside of us. This is where you let it out.

In order to attract people you need to be yourself. You need to remember that people can't relate to your perfection. If you are concerned with being perfect in your videos instead of being raw and real, or better yet vulnerable, you won't attract people.

Before reading the options below, I need to caution you. There are so many ideas, and so many different ways to attract people. I seriously could write a separate book of just ideas for Attraction Pillar™ options. So just use caution when reading the ideas below. Please don't start doing all of them. You will spin your wheels and it will hurt your business. Okay?

Let's look at some Attraction Pillar™ options.

Option #1: YouTube Channel Focused

The first option is to build a YouTube channel. As I write this book, this is currently my favorite Attraction Pillar™. It's my favorite because it's the one that seems to produce the most results for agents. The recipe for this option is clear and easy to follow—just like a paint-by-number set.

When building a YouTube channel you need to focus on keywords to match what people are searching for. What are people searching for? Information about moving to your area! For example, if someone searched "Moving to Madison WI," they most likely are moving to Madison, WI. Why else would you search that? You create a video that satisfies that search. Your video would include all the things you need to know if you are moving to Madison, such as weather, transportation, school districts, etc. Other popular videos include:

- Living in [your city]
- Cost of Living in [your city]
- Pros and Cons of Living in [your city]
- Living in [your city] vs. [another city]

And the list goes on.[25]

Option #2: Niche Social Media Ecosystem

The second option is to focus on a niche and start a social media ecosystem around this niche. Niches could include first-time buyers, senior living, military, vacation rentals, divorce, probate, investors, and so on—depending on your area of focus. Once you've chosen your niche, ask yourself, "What are these people looking for? What is their

---

25 Agent Rise members have access to this list and many more templates inside Agent Rise Coaching. Go to agentrisecoaching.com to learn more.

felt need?" For example, with first-time buyers, down payment assistance (DPA) is a felt need. Here's an approach that has worked well as a lead magnet for this group—a free post inside Facebook Marketplace explaining how grants and down payment assistance programs are now available. We use this to start a conversation, gather information, connect them with a lender, and begin the process of working with them. If they're not quite ready to buy, we invite them to join our first-time buyer Facebook group. Then each month we conduct first-time buyer webinars. It's all about bringing them into the ecosystem, educating them, and encouraging them all the way up until the time they are ready to buy a house.

Option #3: Social Agent Plan

The third option is what we call the Social Agent Plan. If you choose this, then you are saying, "I love social media, I want to be loud, I want to be the digital mayor of my town, and I want to be a media company that happens to sell real estate." You use 1-3 social platforms—Facebook, Instagram, maybe TikTok—and your goal is to be "everywhere." You manage a calendar of scheduled posts. You post just listed, just sold, at a closing with a buyer/seller. Sprinkle in real life, family, personal struggles (with appropriate vulnerability). You talk life, talk real estate, talk community. You might feature a weekly show using Facebook live, or a weekly game of some sort. I used this approach for a while and featured Mathweg Monday Trivia, and achieved high levels of engagement.

Option #4: One Platform Focused (Instagram, LinkedIn)

The fourth option is to pick a platform like Instagram, LinkedIn, or TikTok and focus on it. For example, Paul Wolfert in Michigan (@paulwolfert) has made Instagram his main focus. He always has a story going. He includes you in his journey. He is always talking about real estate, but in a fun way. He is creative and funny. And as a result has drawn an audience and following of 4K. He is yet to buy a lead. By focusing on storytelling, his business has exploded.

Option #5: Podcasting with Social Agent Plan

The fifth option is podcasting along with being a Social Agent. Matt Weber in Dunwoody GA started a podcast called *What's Up Dunwoody*, where he produces a weekly show highlighting Dunwoody. This has gained him a huge following, interviews with city officials, Georgia Attorney General, GA House Representatives, spots recorded by city media directors, and even a TED TALK speaker. Besides the big names, local small businesses are really what the focus is on. That's what's most important about what he does. It has even earned Matt a spot as the parade director of Dunwoody's 4th of July Parade, the largest in Georgia.

Option #6: Blogging with Social Agent Plan

The sixth option is blogging. I think this is where a lot of agents started their attraction pillar back in the day. Today, with YouTube and social media coming onto the scene, blogging has been pushed back in popularity, but it doesn't mean that it doesn't work. If your strength is writing, then blogging could be for you and you shouldn't ignore it. With blogging comes email marketing. You constantly want to be growing your list of readers and emailing them with new blog posts. Headlines and subject lines matter here. Track your opens and clicks. Experiment with different lengths and formats to find out what resonates most with your audience.

Option #7: Other

Your Attraction Pillar™ is limited only by your creativity. You may have a breakthrough idea that isn't listed here. If so, go for it. And tell me about it—I would love to learn from you!

A word about video

If you're like most agents, you feel like you need to produce video. You may have gotten the message: Any type of video will do. You have been told to create content to get attention. It's an attention game that we are all playing. The more attention you get the more deals you will have.

You may have seen posts describing the five types of videos you "should" be making:

1. Property videos
2. Community videos

3. Interview business owners

4. Market reports

5. Tips for consumers

Like I explained in Mary's story, these videos are good, but you can take the same energy, get more focused, produce "living in" or "moving to" videos on a YouTube channel, and get far better results.

Here's an example: Bern McGovern in San Diego came to the Agent Rise Summit in the fall of 2019. Bern was producing videos similar to what I was doing with my *I Love Madison* series. We were interviewing the business owners and non-profit directors, documenting the events and happenings of our cities. As Bern and I shared our notes, we saw the same thing. We were getting about 200–300 views on YouTube because we were driving traffic from social. But our channels were not picking up organic views from people searching for real estate. We were both spinning are wheels with our channels. But when Karin Carr appeared on my podcast, she explained how she was using a different approach to build her YouTube channel. Bern and I exchanged notes, and we both decided it would be best to listen to Karin. Bern left the Summit, went back to San Diego, and changed the focus of his YouTube Channel. He no longer put his energy into becoming a digital mayor (doing community videos). Instead he shifted all of his attention to "living in San Diego," "pros and cons to living in San Diego," "cost of living in San Diego," and "moving to San Diego" style videos. At the writing of this book, Bern's top video has 47K views, and he just reached 5,000 subscribers to his channel. But has he sold any houses? You bet he has! In 2020, he finished the year with $11MM in sales just from YouTube. And half way through 2021, he has already exceeded that number, plus has a huge pipeline of buyers waiting to get into houses. To say it's working is an understatement. This is a prime example of using the same energy for videos, but getting far better results.

As you can see, the Three Pillar approach creates plenty of space for you to be who you are. There's something here for every personality, and plenty of room for you to express your own individuality.

At the same time, the Three Pillar approach works. I've used this approach to help many floundering real estate agents to turn their business around and see the success that had previously eluded them.

26. Work according to your vision

When you have a clear plan, you can work according to your vision. Most agents do the opposite; they work according to their needs.

I get it, you NEED a paycheck. That makes it very tempting to try something for a few weeks or months, and if you don't see results, you stop and get working on something else. After all, you need a paycheck, right?

But here's the problem: Switching to something else is what's going to prevent you from getting that paycheck you need. There is a cost in switching, and that cost prolongs the process of getting paid.

Let's look at it another way: You never fail at something unless you quit. When you invest your energy toward a goal, you either get results or a lesson. And if you get a lesson, you can work smarter next time. You stack up those lessons until you reach the results you're looking for. If you quit, if you abandon ship, and go do something else, you now just wiped out all of your lessons.

Agents who work according to their needs make foolish decisions. They flirt with failure because they quit. They lose out on all the lessons they've stacked up, and they find themselves starting over month after month, but never achieve the results they're looking for.

On the other hand, when you work according to your vision, you have clarity and confidence (maybe borrowed confidence in the beginning) to keep stacking up lessons until you reach results.

Also, when working according to a vision, you'll have more pep in your step. You'll be energized, and more excited to work every day. You know where you are going.

Having a clear plan is just one part of working according to a vision. An important part, but still just one part. The main drive to working according to a vision is your dreams, your goals, what you're working for. With that we encourage agents to write a Vivid Vision Statement. A statement that lays out where you are going. We have found that if you know where you are going and if you have that end in sight, you will reach for that vision and work with more passion and fire.

We all have the ability to do ten times—maybe 50 times—what we are doing right now. Most of us don't believe that. Most people feel they are at capacity and those that produce more are better than they are. I just don't buy that. I believe we all have the ability to do more.

I also believe that producing more doesn't necessarily come by more effort. You don't need to work 80 hours a week and leave your life behind. This isn't a "hustle more" book! On the contrary. I recommend you set boundaries. It may seem counter intuitive, but I've seen agent after agent produce more once they set boundaries—once they limit how much time they will spend on real estate. I believe in boundaries, and I believe in receiving the abundance that has been provided for us. We just need to align our vision and remove our limiting beliefs.

I want to help you build a vivid vision of your future so that you can call out your limiting beliefs.

I enjoyed reading *The Ant and The Elephant* by Vince Poscente. According to the author, our minds are separated into two distinct spaces—conscious and subconscious thought. Our "ant" is the intentional part of the brain—it houses our critical, analytical thoughts. Our "elephant," however, is the instructional, impulsive part of the brain—it houses emotions and memories and even guides the body to perform its vital functions. While we tend to know our conscious minds—our ants—rather well, we often overlook the power of our elephantine subconscious minds. Unfortunately, when we do, we squander a wellspring of human potential.

Imagine a tiny ant on the back of a massive elephant. No matter how diligently that ant marches east, if the elephant he sits upon travels in the opposite direction, the ant will end up even farther west then his starting point.

So I want to help you align both your conscious and your subconscious minds. I want you to dream, and I want you to weed out those limiting beliefs.

I have done this so many times in my life. I create a vision in my mind of where I want to go and what I want to do. Take my first podcast, Onion Juice Podcast, for example. I had a vision for it, and I knew that I would help a lot of people. I had doubters the entire way. I still have people, to this day, who poke fun at me about the name, or show, or the fact that I take my podcast as seriously as I do. You're going to have that and many times you have to go back to your original vision to see how far you've come. Often, you've gone further then you ever dreamed and it's time to up the goal.

Are you afraid of dreaming big?

Vivid Vision Statements are designed to give you direction. So dream big!

Keep in mind that a Vivid Vision Statement is not a mission statement. A mission statement is to help customers and teammates understand your company and its beliefs. Vision statements point to the future. When writing your vivid vision, pretend you have arrived at the place you want to be. Describe what that looks like.

Your goal is to have a concise vision statement—anywhere from a sentence to a paragraph. However, in the beginning, this statement will start out longer.

Step 1. Dream big and focus on success. Walk through your day as if it is everything you wish for. From the car you're driving, to what your office looks like, to how many people are in your office, to the setup of your team. Just dream away and write it all down. We live in a world of abundance. We just need to receive it.

Step 2. Align your ant and elephant—your conscious and subconscious minds. Remove all of those limiting beliefs. What roadblocks did you run into? For example, did you catch yourself saying something like, "If I grow that big, then I would need a team. I don't know how to hire, I don't want the risk of hiring someone?" If so, then this is the same story that your subconscious mind is going to tell to prevent yourself from the growth you dream to achieve. Instead, write down: "I will learn how to hire by surrounding myself with others who have. I will minimize the risk and hire slowly, and I will build great systems so others can jump in when needed." See what we're doing here. Aligning the ant and elephant. Getting them both to go the same direction.

Step 3. Take your final big dream and trim it down to a page. This page should be a summary of the details. This is the page that you'll want to read often.

Step 4. Believe it and watch it happen. Journal it. Remember what I said in the beginning—we all have the ability to do ten times what we are doing right now and when we fight through that resistance it's amazing how easy that next level becomes.

Today I truly believe in God's abundance and believe He has already given it to us and we just have to receive.

After my wife and I lost it all in the recession, we agreed to pay back $264,000. Talk about a hard time believing in abundance! But it was in those times that I received it the most. 2011 was the worst year of my career according to my income. But looking back on it, we received so much abundance. For example, we found a car for $500 that looked nice and ran like a champ. An old friend from high school heard we were struggling and wanted to give us $2000. One morning as I left to deliver newspapers (a side hustle to bring in some cash), I discovered four bags full of toys on our porch for our kids for Christmas.

During my darkest days, I received all of that. So if you're in your darkest days I beg you to stop and think, look around you, and see all the abundance. I would have never thought a $500 car would be called abundance until I had no car at all. Believe me there is abundance around you.

Today, I'm living out another vision. I bought an RV and I'm traveling the country with my wife and family. Along the way, I meet with real estate agents in city after city.

So no matter where you're at in your career, dream big, remove those lies, align your subconscious and conscious mind and receive the abundance that is out there for you.

27. Discover your power

I believe you have hidden powers that need to be revealed. The best thing about you... is you. You have something no one else has. What are those powers and how do we find them? That is what we are going to uncover in this section of the book.

When I started as a real estate agent, I was 23 years old. I was the young guy in the office. It was hard to get people to put their trust in me because of my age. That was stacked against me and something I struggled to overcome until I stepped into my own power.

What was my power? I knew people. A lot of people. When I was a senior in high school, I started my own small business that introduced me to hundreds.

Here's how it happened:

Our school won the conference football championship my senior year. On the bus ride home from the game someone mentioned that we need t-shirts. Something prompted me to say, "I'll take care of that!" The next morning I went down to a local screen printing shop. We designed a shirt. Then we came up with terms of how I could afford to buy them, and put the order in.

I had to buy 144 of them in order to get the best price.

Brian, the owner of the shop, gave me 30 days to pay him. I had to sell 70% of the shirts in order to break even. I remember being super nervous about the risk, but I just plowed through the fear.

A few days later the shirts were ready for pickup. The next day I went to school with a 144 shirts. I set up shop in the lunchroom. And two days later I was completely sold out!! I went back to Brian with the money 28 days early and I ordered another 144. I did that over and over. If I remember correctly, we sold over 1,000 of those shirts. It was a hit, and it was the beginning of my entrepreneurship journey.

Brian found a power in me and encouraged me to start my own business. By the beginning of my final semester of my senior year, I started my own business. I even ran my business as a part of a work/school coop. I went to school in the morning and ran my business in the afternoon.

I went door to door visiting small businesses—and some big businesses—selling company swag.

I ran the business for six years, until I sold my ownership to pursue real estate full time.

Over those six years I built a database of 300 people in my hometown. The day I became a real estate agent I mailed out my announcement letter to let everyone know I have become a real estate agent. I stepped into my power of having a great database of customers who came to love my service and cheered me on as I continued in my entrepreneurial journey.

The next power I stumbled upon was doing open houses in my hometown where I knew so many people. It all happened one day at a company business meeting. One of the company's top listing agents was complaining about doing open houses. After the meeting I went up to her and asked if I could hold her listings open. For three years I did an open house almost every weekend for this agent and other agents in the office.

People from the community would walk into these open houses and say, "Neil! What are you doing here!?" I would laugh and say, "I'm a real estate agent now!" They would be surprised, but then would say, "Awesome! Can you help us find a house?"

Next thing you know I was out showing them houses. I did this weekend after weekend. I stepped into one of my powers and never looked back. This worked for me because it was my power. Let's find yours!

When finding your power, you might think of taking Tom Rath's *Strengths Finder* test or a personality test like Myers-Briggs. Those tests are good, but it's not what we are looking for in discovering your powers. One of your powers is your personality, but that is only one. We want to look beyond that when discovering your power.

Finding your super power is about what you think you bring to the table and how you see yourself. To identify your powers, we'll look at these eight categories:

1) Company powers

2) Community powers (groups and relationships)

3) Technical powers

4) Social powers

5) Organizational powers

6) Communication powers

7) Financial powers

8) Leadership powers

Let's take a closer look.

#1 Company powers

Powers within your company or firm: If you are a part of a firm that has hundreds of agents, you will be swimming in opportunities for open houses. However, if you are a part of a boutique office, you will struggle with open houses as your Chase Pillar™. It's not impossible, but it's going to be an uphill battle to find enough open houses. On the other hand your boutique office might offer online leads. Some boutiques are setup like teams and offer direct leads to your business. You need to find your strength within your office.

#2 Community powers

Powers within your community, groups, or relationships: Mine came from being a business owner for six years and building a database of customers. But maybe you are a part of the PTA at your children's school, or member of a vibrant chamber of commerce. Sometimes it's large groups, sometimes it's small groups. We want to identify these groups and come up with a plan to help you develop business around them, without feeling salesy. We don't want you walking in with commission breath, that's for sure!

#3 Technical powers

Powers from technical skills: I always say if you're not techy, you shouldn't be doing Facebook ads as your Chase Pillar™. On the contrary if you can geek out about the latest techniques and strategies to maximize results, then you should consider it. Never feel like you need to know it all, but if you have some skills there or confidence, then you can build those skills, and it's best for you to step into that power.

#4 Social powers

If you are an extrovert you should have a great time with social media or networking events. Open houses will also fuel you. If you are introverted you might love online leads or Facebook Ads for your chase and YouTube for your attraction. Yes, you read that right. YouTube for your attraction, because it needs you to be detail oriented to provide the detailed information the viewer is looking for. I remember when my good friend Joe Marks was thinking about starting a YouTube channel he was afraid to because he wasn't extroverted, outgoing, and bubbly. He was afraid he would be too dry and not entertaining enough for YouTube.

I encouraged Joe to look at it differently and to understand that what YouTube viewers are looking for are details and answers to their questions. Being Joe's good friend I always noticed that I could never tell Joe a story without him asking questions and needing more context to the story. He always wanted more details. It's in his being, and this is the strength he brought to YouTube. So when you hear that most introverts can't make it as real estate agents, I'm here to prove the naysayers wrong. If they struggle, it just means they aren't working according to their super powers.

#5 Organizational powers

Your organizational skills: If you're not very organized, then simplify everything so you have less to organize—or hire an assistant or transaction coordinator to help with organization. If you are organized, then you want to leverage that strength.

#6 Communication powers

What communication skills, writing skills, or other powers do you possess that might empower you to reach your audience?

#7 Financial powers

Some of us come into this business with very little money saved to invest into our businesses. Others are on stronger financial footing. This can help you select your approach. For example, if you don't have much money to invest, you might want to select Open Houses as your Chase Pillar™ as that's the cheapest option. If you have a few hundred bucks a month to invest, then you might want to consider Facebook Advertising. If you have even more to invest, then you might get the best return on your investment with online leads. Of course, you need to take into consideration your social powers and other powers when making these decisions.

#8 Leadership powers

If you have a desire to lead, then I would use that in your business in a few ways. First with your sphere, you can lead client events, book clubs, bible studies, and other social events. For your attraction pillar you can lead networking events or meetups. You can also use this power to lead a team or a brokerage. Bottom line if you desire to lead, then by all means cultivate leadership skills, and use this power to lead.

Use your powers to your advantage in building your business. Your business should never look exactly like someone else's because each person possesses different powers. This is the best thing about building a business you love, it's yours and only yours, and it plays to your strengths and only yours.

In Agent Rise Coaching we work to identify your powers and help you build a plan that plays to your strengths. Learn more at www.agentrisecoaching.com.

28. Consistency

Consistency leads to mastery.

When you begin in this business your efforts are going to outweigh your results. Then you'll reach a tipping point where your results will start to outweigh your efforts.

Imagine you're at the top of a hill, and you want to push a big boulder down the hill. Your first attempt to move the boulder will throw you back and make you come at it again. On your second try, you might get the boulder to rock a bit. Then it will rock back and forth. Then maybe you'll get it roll a tad, before it rolls back at you. But you don't give up. Eventually, after rocking it back and forth, you'll get it to roll forward. Then you'll roll it again, and then all of a sudden it begins to roll down the hill with a force you cannot stop. That's what its like to get your business going. Efforts are going to outweigh the results until you reach the tipping point. Then your results are going to outweigh your efforts.

You can only reach those results and mastery if you're consistent. Like Bruce Lee said, "I fear not the man who has practiced 10,000 kicks once, but I fear the man who has practiced one kick 10,000 times."

Most agents don't stay consistent long enough to achieve mastery.

Consider this scenario: You decide to make open houses your Chase Pillar™. In the past, you haven't had much success with open houses—you've sat for hours and never got any business. You feel reluctance and doubt, but you're going to give it a shot because you keep hearing about agents who are crushing it at open houses.

After a couple weeks, you land your first open house. Here goes nothing.

You show up with the property profile sheet, pens, cookies, and bottles of water.

Three groups of people visit. You're excited. Two of them are already working with another agent. They don't sign in even though you ask them to. You try to get a conversation going with the one who doesn't, but it leads to nothing.

The two hours come to an end. Now you need to drive through the neighborhood, pick up all the signs, and then head to your kid's soccer game only to see the last ten minutes of the game.

You feel defeated, and now all you can think is: *Open houses aren't for me.*

A couple weeks go by and another open house opportunity arrives. You take it, only because it's your pillar! You think, *I better stick to my plan.*

This open house is even worse. Two groups come through and both have an agent. Not one good lead out of the entire open house.

Does this sound familiar? The truth is: This is common for the agent who doesn't work in excellence, doesn't stack lessons, and is far from mastery.

Now let's look at what an open house looks like if you are a master at open houses:

First, you are proactive in getting open houses and will do two to three a weekend, and one on Thursday nights.

You direct message listing agents about the specific listing of the house you want to hold open. You don't wait for opportunities to come, instead you go to the opportunity.

You give the listing agent immediate feedback and work to impress the listing agent. This assures you a steady stream of open houses.

You keep your open houses simple so you have energy to meet people. You have a stack of small clipboards in your hand and are ready to hand them out to people as they walk in the door. You hold your post and wait for them to return from their tour.

When the buyer ends their tour, you work on getting the buyer's search criteria. The first question you ask is, "Do you have any questions about or interest in the house?" If they answer "no," now you ask, "So I can give feedback to the seller, what did you like most and what did you like least about the house?" This will get the buyer talking about their search criteria. The buyer will say something like: "We love the back yard and the three-car garage, but we really need to have 4 bedrooms." From that you now know they want a 4 bedroom home with a three-car garage and a nice back yard. From there you can go on to ask more to get the buyer's "story of criteria." If the conversation continues, you can ask, "What are the three must haves you need in your new home?"

Now you have the buyers contact information on the clipboard you handed them, and now you have their search criteria.

You add the buyer to your matchmaker and you begin to call them with a house that matches what they are looking for.

Of course, your plan may or may not include open houses. But whatever your plan is, stick with it. Be consistent. Learn from your mistakes, improve what you do, but don't abandon your plan simply because it takes time to work. Success takes time. It doesn't happen overnight. You need to build a solid foundation and gain the momentum that comes with consistency.

29. Day Blocking

After you get through the first six Agent Rise Steps, you will want to implement Day Blocking. Time blocking never worked for me, and I know it doesn't work for 99% of agents. We don't do time blocking. Instead, we do Day Blocking.

The Day Blocker works better than time blocking, because it helps me stay focused on my clients and my three pillar plan. I just focus on getting this done sometime throughout the day.

It looks like this:

Monday: I call all of my hot leads. These are people that are on my lead tracker that I didn't call last week while matchmaking.

Tuesday: I call and give updates to all clients listed with me or in pending. I tell all my clients I will call them every Tuesday.

Wednesday: I work on my Sphere of Influence Pillar™. It's newsletter day. If I have a client event coming up, it's the day I call my sphere to personally invite them to the event (in addition to the invite I have mailed).

Thursday: I work on my Chase Pillar™. For me it was

open houses, so on Thursday I was setting up signs, ads, and brochures for the opens coming this weekend.

Friday: I worked on my attraction pillar. For me it was my content planning day, writing day, and producing videos and content for the up coming week. I love Fridays!

In addition, every day I looked for off-market properties for 30 minutes a day, called 5 buyers with matches, and I mailed letters to old expireds or neighborhoods for my buyers who can't find a house on the market. This keeps my matchmaking game fresh!

Pro tip: Envision the best environment to make calls to your leads (the best time to reach people) or the place you want to be when making those calls—your office or your car.

30. Self integrity

If you're a good human, you have integrity with others. When we say we are going to be somewhere at a certain time, we'll be there. Or when we tell someone that we'll do something, we do it. When we promise someone something, for the most part we'll follow through with our promises.

But what we sometimes lack—me included—is integrity with ourselves. Have you ever told yourself you were going to do something and then didn't?

I'm going to lose weight—and four days into the diet you fall off. You didn't keep the promise with yourself.

I'm going to matchmake every day five days a week. On Thursday you get busy with a deal, and you don't make the calls. You didn't keep the promise with yourself.

I'm going to mail two thank you cards a day. Friday comes, you had a busy week and it's time to go away for the weekend. You didn't mail your cards. You didn't keep the promise with yourself.

Why do we do this? Because no one is watching. No one knows we didn't do it. Therefore we didn't let anyone down, we didn't lose any integrity with anyone.

Wrong.

We lost integrity with ourselves. When we tell ourselves we're going to do something and don't, we lose belief in ourselves. We lose dignity and we feel so defeated that we stop believing in ourselves. As a result we get stuck and we stop making promises with ourselves.

Our dignity tanks are empty.

The only way to fill them back up is to make small promises with ourselves and accomplish them. So small that they seem stupid...like: *I will brush my teeth first thing in the morning and again before I go to bed*. Or: *I will make my bed in the morning*. Seriously, start there. Get promise momentum going. Then add more promises. One step at a time until you begin to fill that dignity tank.

Then once you have some promise momentum going, it's time to take that into your business and have the discipline to carry it out and keep going.

When you bring this to your business, start small again. Make sure your promises are around efforts (or tasks) and not around results. For example, I do not promise myself I'm going to get one accepted offer a week. That's a result from the efforts, and I do not have 100% control over results. Instead, I might promise myself that I'm going to call 5 buyers a day to tell them about houses I found for them. That's a promise I can keep.

Pro tip: If you find yourself needing extra support, get creative. For example, can you ask a family member to help with your thank yous? Maybe it's their jam.

31. Set boundaries

As you grow your business you can often find yourself losing your life. You can give so much to the business that there is nothing left for you and your family.

I was going 100 mph and was working about 70-80 hours a week. I realized I had a problem so I started to not schedule anything for Sundays. I didn't tell my clients; I just dodged the appointments. (That was a big mistake, and I'll show you how to do it the right way in a minute.) But there was this one Sunday that I will never forget. I took the day off, and we went to the zoo as a family. My daughter Natalie was 5 at the time. We had a great day. As I was tucking her into bed, she looked at me and said, "Dad, what a great day!"

I said, "Yeah, Sweetie, it sure was a great day, wasn't it?"

Then she said, "I'll see you next Sunday".

It hit me so hard! That's how absent I was. She seriously looked forward to Sundays for the possibility that I would take a day off work.

I lost it that night. Right there I decided I had to change. The next morning I posted the story on Facebook. I called all of my clients and told them I needed to set boundaries and needed to take Sundays off, and I needed to be done working every day by 6 pm.

After that, whenever I met with a new client, I said this at the end of our first meeting: "There is one more thing I would like to go over with you, and that is that I don't work on Sundays. I guard that day for church and family. I also need to be home by 6 pm every night for my family. Is that okay with you?" Since doing this in 2010, I have had one person say no, otherwise every single person has said, "Yes, no problem."

Most are afraid to do this, because they are afraid they will push people away. But here is the truth: It doesn't push people away. Instead, it attracts them. When you set boundaries, you begin to earn their respect. When you earn someone's respect, you will begin to earn their referrals. People don't refer people they don't respect.

I also hear new agents say, they will worry about that when they get busy. Please don't follow that advice. Set your boundaries now so you start earning people's trust now. Don't fall into the trap of the disease to please. Once you start down that path, it's hard to stop. You can serve people with excellence without sacrificing your time with your family or your time for yourself. When you take time out to renew, you place yourself in a position to serve them even better. Guard that now before it gets out of control.

All of my clients respected my day off. They never called, or never requested a showing, on Sunday. If there was a Sunday open house, they went without me. They never requested an evening showing or expected me to write an offer late at night. Instead, they left work early to see houses. They respected me; they respected my family.

I have helped many agents set boundaries, but there is one agent I will never forget. She came into my office one morning in tears. She had grown her business and now it was out of control. She had a very bad case of the disease to please. She had an evening this last week where she had no appointments. She told her family she would be home by 5 pm, they would have their favorite dinner, and they would have a fun movie night together as a family.

That didn't go as planned. As she was cooking dinner a buyer called. They had seen a house earlier, and they now decided they wanted to write an offer. They were first-time buyers, and had no understanding of the process. On top of that, they were extremely nervous and rightfully wanted to understand everything.

So she answered the call and said, "Great, let's get this offer submitted for you." She asked her husband to take over cooking dinner while she went into the bedroom to write the offer for this couple. She said it will take about 30 minutes to write the offer and dinner should be done in about the same time.

Well, that didn't go as planned either. She found herself in the bedroom for three hours writing the offer. Twice she had to stop to yell at the kids who were knocking on the door to tell her dinner was ready and another time to tell her that they were starting the movie. When she finally finished the call she came out to the living room to see dinner put away, her husband sleeping on the couch, and her kids in bed. She missed the entire night.

She came to my office that next morning with tears in her eyes. She said, "I can't do this anymore!"

We then talked about what she needed to do differently. First, she had never set any expectations with her clients. They had no idea what she was missing out on by writing this offer. If they did, they probably would have called her at 2 or 3 pm instead of after 5 pm. Or they may have waited until the next morning. Or they would have let her know that tomorrow is fine to write the offer. We must remember *we train our clients*. She trained them to think she has no life and is always there for her clients. That is not healthy.

Once those boundaries are in place, she could have said, "I am with my family tonight. Kids go to bed at 8 pm, and I can write your offer then. In the meantime, I'm going to send you an email with questions. Read the email and respond to the questions. I will then take this to draft your offer at 8 pm." Alternatively, they could sign the offer in the morning if there was time—in this case there was time.

When you set boundaries, you make room for your family and for yourself. You don't push people away you draw them closer. They will respect you, and they won't ask for anything that doesn't respect the boundaries you place. As a result, you will grow your business, and you will gain the time you and your family need. I promise you: you won't regret it.

32. Information alone doesn't work

In this book, you've gained plenty of good information.

But information alone won't get you where you want to go.

I believe you can build a business you love. I believe your can have an amazing career. I believe your breakthrough is right around the corner, that you can succeed as a real estate agent.

But information alone won't get you any of these things.

We are in the middle of the information era and we have information in abundance. In this book, I've shared a lot of information with you—maybe even too much. You might feel like you are drinking from a fire hose. You will need to decide what works for you—what you need, how it applies to you, and where you are in building your business.

Yet here's the truth: Information alone won't get you to where you want to go.

But coaching will.

Coaching means you value yourself, you're worth the investment. Coaching works because we learn with action, not thought alone. And learning in community is another huge reason to join a group coaching program.

Coaching gets you to the level you want to achieve. You need someone to analyze your strengths with you to help you build your clear plan. You need accountability to actually build your clear plan. You need someone to spot and remove limiting beliefs that block your progress. You need a sounding board to discuss ideas and conquer challenges. You need a mindset shift on the days you feel down and have thoughts of quitting.

Can you imagine if an athlete didn't have a coach? Most likely, they know the tactics to play the sport, but they would never grow in excellence without a coach helping them. Most professional athletes have three or four coaches surrounding them.

I have surrounded myself with coaches throughout my career, and—without them—there is no way I would be where I am today.

Having the right coach matters. Remember our story. Mary had "coaches" in her office. But they weren't helping her. In the same way, you will want to watch out for bad advice coming from people who think they know. They may have great intentions and mean well in helping you. But that doesn't mean they know what you need.

You've probably heard this: "Take advice from those who are doing what you want to do." But here's the problem many of us in real estate run into: We take advice from agents who have succeeded in this business. While that might sound like a good idea, it often doesn't work. Here's why: Most of them don't even know how they did it or if they did it because they had a superpower that you don't. So you listen to them, and you try to build your business like they did, however it's not working because you don't have what they have. You need to work from your strengths, not from theirs. These successful agents may have great intentions and may mean well in helping you, but that doesn't mean they know what you need.

You might be like some agents who haven't hired a coach because you have some fears. You'll find yourself saying things like:

"Am I going to be able to handle the work that the coach requires me to do?"

"I'd rather just grow slowly, I don't want to be too busy!"

"What if it works, and I can't handle the business?"

Do you know what all of these statements have in common? They all bring up fears of success.

Fear of success? Wait, isn't success what we all want? Yes it is, but when you think about going to heights you dream of going to, you get afraid. You're not ready for that climb yet.

But here is the thing, a good coach knows that and empowers you to conquer those fears one step at a time.

You never arrive in this business. But that doesn't mean you're stuck where you are. Your breakthrough is waiting for you. You can move forward.

How do you move forward?

Together.

No one succeeds in this business alone. We all need help. Here at Agent Rise, we would like to be on your team. We would like to be part of your success.

Remember: *What got you here, will not get you there*. But when you surround yourself with the right people (and a coach being one of them) the information, confidence, and resources you need to get there will be there for you when you need it.

One step at a time.

If you want to get there, and you're looking for a coach to come alongside of you, we at Agent Rise would like to apply. We'd like to see you implement everything in this book along with much more to grow a business you love and breakthrough to heights you never thought were possible.

Make one promise to yourself: Schedule a coaching discovery call at agentrisecoaching.com. It's free. It's 30 minutes. And it will change your business and change your life. I guarantee it, or your money back! ☺

Free Resources

Visit agentrisecoaching.com/resources for any of these free resources:

Three Pillar Plan™

Agent Rise Steps™

"Secrets to Winning Listings"

"Buyer Expired Letter Email Template"

"Price Adjustment Resource"

"Open House Sign-in Sheet"

"Buyer Accepted Offer Email Template"

Here's to the Risers

As you launch your journey, I want to share the Riser's Creed with you. I wrote this for our Agent Rise members as I see so many of them fight to their breakthrough and beyond. I also wrote this for you, as your anthem to your break through.

> Here's to the Risers.
> To the fighters
> the survivors,
> the stay up all-nighters.
> The ones with desire,
> with fire,
> who want to inspire.
> You can't ignore them.
> They won't back down.
> They won't give up.
> They are a Riser.
>
> They know what they need to do.
> They have a clear plan.
> They work according to a vision.
> They avoid shiny objects.
> They are consistent.

They are 100% responsible,
failure isn't possible.
They are a Riser.

They know the door is revolving.
That won't stop them.
They know the odds are against them.
They don't care.
They follow the steps.
They work with confidence.
And at the end of the day,
They know they are well on their way.
They are a Riser.

Schedule a coaching discovery call at agentrisecoaching.com. It's free. It's 30 minutes. And it will change your business and change your life. I guarantee it, or your money back! 😊

Made in the USA
Middletown, DE
19 January 2025

68968640R00096